MOTHER GOOSE

By Florence Rogers

with Princella D. Smith

Beauty For Ashes
Triumph Over Tragedy

Beauty for Ashes Book Series Volume 2

Beauty For Ashes
Triumph Over Tragedy

Beauty for Ashes Book Series Volume 2

Mother Goose Bombing Book, LLC

Authored by Florence Rogers
Edited and Co-Authored by: Princella D. Smith

Table Of Contents

Foreword

More than 25 years have passed since the bombing in Oklahoma City.

Florence Rogers known by many who love her as Mother Goose, has lived her life in respectful remembrance of the people killed in the blast including 18 beautiful women who served as her employees at the Federal Employees Credit Union.

Mother Goose grew up on the countryside of rural Minco, Oklahoma, approximately 45 miles from Oklahoma City. During her life on the farm, nature was many times her only friend. She especially enjoyed watching the geese that were often present because the local farmers planted wheat, and the geese loved the fresh growth of the grain.

Since the tragic blast, regardless of where she may be, when a formation of geese fly across the sky, Mother Goose literally freezes in her tracks, watches the flight until they are completely out of sight, and remarks: "There go my girls!"

The creation of this book was an emotional experience for Mother Goose as it has caused her to revisit every aspect of the tragic day and its aftermath: all of the goodbyes; all of the grief of the families who sought her counsel through their loss and through the rebuilding of their financial futures.

In this book, you will get to know Florence Rogers, and how she lived her life. Many call her Mother Goose, but I am blessed to call her "Mom."

--Terry Rose

Dedication

To my precious family who flew very quickly to check on their "Mother Goose" after the bombing.

To the eighteen of my little flock at the Federal Employees Credit Union who unexpectedly dropped out of the formation to fly to a brand new destination.

To my two great sons, and the precious ones that they have added to our formation.

--Florence Rogers, Your "MOTHER GOOSE"

Endorsements

"Having Florence Rogers come into my life has been such a gift. And now she has given us all the gift of her story. How she mentally survived the very difficult aftermath of the Oklahoma City bombing is a story we all need to understand. She guided many, including me as a fellow survivor, through our darkest days.

Florence became an impactful voice as Oklahoma City gathered together to memorialize what happened and, ultimately, to help other communities learn from our experience through our Memorial and Museum.

As you read the book, you will understand why our response to the bombing is now known as the Oklahoma Standard. But best of all, you will get to know and understand this special woman."

Polly Nichols, Oklahoma Hall of Famer, Philanthropist

"Florence Rogers tells me often of the important role that Tinker Federal Credit Union played in the recovery of the Federal Employees Credit Union.

We truly welcomed the opportunity to be part of the role of the entire credit union industry in Oklahoma, and elsewhere, played in helping all of us return to a sense of normalcy. I was so impressed to see the giving and cooperative spirit portrayed by everyone.

God blessed us all and pulled Florence, her remaining team, and all of us through this historic tragedy."

Mike Kloiber
Tinker Federal Credit Union President / CEO

Mother Goose

"Florence Rogers lost 18 of her 33 workers at the Federal Employees Credit Union on the third floor of the Alfred P. Murrah Building when the downtown Oklahoma City building was destroyed by a truck bomb 25 years ago.

Since then, she has spoken to countless groups and businesses in the United States and around the world providing insights on how to cope with unthinkable loss and triumph. Now Rogers, a survivor of the bombing, is paying tribute to the workers whose lives were cut short by domestic terrorist Timothy McVeigh. It is yet another gift to all of us from this remarkable woman."

Lou Michel, co-author of
New York Times Best Seller, American Terrorist: Timothy McVeigh and the Oklahoma City Bombing

"Covering the Murrah Federal building bombing was a life changer and a career milestone.

The epic story of Florence Rogers and her gals...her beloved "geese" at the Credit union amid such staggering loss...became a kernel of recovery and hope, an example of strength and resilience for the entire OKC community -- and the nation--for months and years to come. "

Brian O'Keefe, Producer
"48 Hours" CBS News, "Good Morning America" ABC

"Florence Rogers is a rare woman. She was head of the Federal Employees Credit Union at a time when women executives were scarce. Florence earned the position with resilience, courage and compassion.

She would need all of those strengths on April 19, 1995. Her story is compelling—as are the lessons we can learn from her."

Linda Cavanaugh
Emmy Award-winning Broadcast Journalist

Chapter 1
Get Up

A concussive force of wind ripped me from my desk and flung me against the wall in a tornado-like rush.

When I came to my senses, I was surrounded by cement, boulders, twisted wires, and steel beams. Concrete dust and smoke blurred my vision, but I could see daylight where my office ceiling used to be, and my desk hung over the edge of what was left of the floor.

It smelled as if the building was on fire. Where had my staff gone? ***Why did they leave me here***?

Later I would learn that the same concussive wind had hurled them to their deaths below with the six floors above us piled on top of them.

I was the only survivor of my meeting that day.

Why I Wrote Mother Goose

Have you ever been knocked on your back? The force of an attack, an ailment, or just a slip of your foot leaves you lying there—possibly in pain. You're left with two choices: lie there or get ***up***. Even if you've suffered debilitating injuries, the paramedics' first step will be to pick you ***up*** off the floor and onto a stretcher to get you to the hospital.

Thousands of people have heard my story of survival of the Oklahoma City Bombing, America's largest domestic terrorist attack. Without fail, at least one person in every audience wants to know: "How did you make it? How did you get through the grief of losing 18 employees? How did you overcome the trauma of nearly being killed?"

My answer? I got ***up***! No matter what life does to throw you down, you have to get up. Even if you need help getting up, the point is that you ***get up.***

I never met Dr. Craig Lounsbrough, but had I known of his counseling literature, I might have been able to answer this question more effectively.

This quote of his sums it up: *"If I get up just one less time than the number of times I've been knocked down, I have done one of the most devastating things possible; I have halted my life at that very spot."*

If you're a sports fan, you might like Sylvester Stallone's quote in his film, Balboa, the 6th installment of the Rocky film series:

"Let me tell you something you already know. The world ain't all sunshine and rainbows.

"It's a very mean and nasty place, and I don't care how tough you are, it will beat you to your knees and keep you there permanently if you let it. You, me, or nobody is gonna hit as hard as life. But it ain't about how hard you hit.

"It's about how hard you can get hit and keep moving forward; how much you can take and keep moving forward."

On April 19, 1995, I went from managing a credit union in one of Oklahoma City's most prominent buildings, to being knocked on my back with broken vertebrae, leg wounds, and the back side of my body riddled in severe bruises.

I didn't know it at the time, but the concussive force of a madman's bomb had not only physically knocked me down, but it would lead to the biggest emotional, spiritual, and mental tests of my life.

My physical recovery process would be the least of my challenges as I would be faced with the trauma of losing 18 of my 33 beloved employees, the shared grief of mourning with their families and surviving co-workers, and the mentally taxing toll of rebuilding a financial institution, important to so many, that had been laid to rubble.

I wrote Mother Goose to perhaps encourage others to understand that no matter what life throws at you—and boy did it throw me one heck of a storm—you *can* get back up again. You *can* get through it, and you will certainly place a more precious value on this beautiful fragile experience we call life.

***

The Day Of The Horrible Bombing

I really loved my job as CEO of the Federal Employees Credit Union.

It was more than my source of income. It was more than the tangibles of a company car and a corner office on the third floor of Oklahoma City's prominent Alfred P. Murrah Building.

It was a part of my identity.

My 33 employees weren't just "people who worked for me" but men and women who were part of a larger family. This was especially true with the women of the office. They were like my sisters and daughters. We celebrated each others' life milestones such as birthdays, babies, and even cancer survivals creating a truly unique atmosphere of family. That is why losing 18 of those women was so incredibly devastating.

I reveal heartwarming stories about our relationships and my grieving / recovery process over these special ladies in chapter 2.

On the morning of the bombing, Wednesday, April 19, 1995, I made it a point to arrive at the office early. I had been out for a week on a cruise with my sister, Joellyn. We'd had such a great time, and I had needed that break. Feeling refreshed and eager to get back in the work saddle, I energetically returned to the office.

Our credit union was always bustling. From opening hour at 9am until closing hour at 5pm, there were people everywhere.

The Murrah Building was located right in the middle of busy, downtown Oklahoma City, and the Federal Employees Credit Union was located on the 3rd floor. Not only did employees at the federal agencies on the other 8 floors have accounts with us, but so did hundreds of others downtown and throughout Oklahoma City.

Several of them would drop by, withdraw cash for their lunch, chat with our employees, and then head one floor higher to the snack bar and socialize there.

Sometimes, they would stop by just to visit with our employees. It was like a big "credit union kitchen table" with multiple conversations, stories, and smiles all over the place.

That Wednesday was no exception. The reason I'd arrived around 8am was to get an early jump on the 8:30am meeting I had scheduled with my department heads. We had several items to cover including preparation for the pending banking department audit, and I wanted enough time to also share my cruise photos.

On top of which, it was one of my best employee's, Sonja Sanders', first day as a department head. With me having been out a week and her stepping into her new position, I had an extra incentive for the meeting to start on time and for every minute to be used efficiently.

Upon entering the office, I was greeted with the familiar hustle and bustle of my employees preparing for the day. I headed straight for my computer and pulled up the department head meeting agenda.

We had just added a new boardroom on the north wall of our beautiful 75 million dollar credit union, and I was looking forward to using it. However, the printer in the boardroom refused to work (as printers like to do whenever you really need them or are in a hurry), so we decided to move the meeting to my office.

I later discovered that this move of the meeting probably saved my life because the catastrophic bomb completely obliterated that board room. However, at the time, I was disappointed. After all the hype of the fancy new space, I really wanted to meet in there. It even seemed like my department heads dressed for the special occasion of meeting in the new space!

The immediate past Sunday had been Easter, so I wondered if they all broke out their brightly colored Easter suits from just three days prior. Nowadays, the private sector is a lot more casual than it was when I ran the credit union. Many present-day companies do not require business attire or even have much of a dress code at all.

At the credit union, my board members and I felt that our outward presentation was an integral part of our professionalism and customer service, and that meant business casual clothing, but even for "back then," I was considered a bit more traditional or hard-nosed in this regard.

I always noticed what my employees wore to work—especially those in senior positions. Don't get me wrong. I wasn't a name "brand snob" because I knew that even with the smallest of pockets, a person could make their wardrobe look nice and well-put-together by keeping it cleaned, pressed, color coordinated, and modestly accessorized.

This included my particular affinity for makeup.

To me, makeup was the perfect complimentary accessory to a sharp-dressed woman's outfit. A point of humor around the office was centered on this notion.

Whenever an employee would say to me: “Mother Goose, I don’t feel good.” I would respond with: “Well, go put on some lipstick, and see how you feel after that.”

I would probably get into some human resources trouble for that today, but that’s how much of an impact I felt that a person’s attire and appearance had on their frame of mind. If you look better, you feel better. A sharp-dressed employee has a confidence boost, and they usually have a more optimal performance.

All this to say: I loved to see my ladies at their absolute best. It was my first and last time seeing each department head in the perfect combination of attire and lipstick. Most of them had closed casket funerals, so this particular morning was the last time I laid eyes on them, and I’m grateful that in my final memory of them, they were in their most quintessential forms.

Just moments before we started the meeting and minutes before the bomb, my Vice President of Finance, Claudette Meek, said: “Look at all of us. We look like a basket of Easter eggs, don’t we!” She always had a daily joke or quip. It was the last one she told, but it might have been the most important one she ever told because it did prompt me to give everyone one more look.

I didn't realize it at the time, but my special attention to their wardrobes also enabled me to tell each one of their family members what each of them were wearing, and it contributed to the first responders' search and rescue efforts in the recovery of their bodies.

By 8:40am, all seven of the sharp-dressed department heads, coffee cups and notepads in hand, had circled my desk in just as neat and orderly a fashion as the ceramic geese collection that adorned my desk. I had personally hired and professionally groomed each of these elegant ladies: Claudette Meek, VP of Finance; Kathy Finley, VP of Operations; Jamie Genzer, General Office Assistant; Sonja Sanders, Chief Teller; Victoria "Vicky" Texter, VISA Program Manager; Valerie Koelsch, Director of Marketing; and Jill Randolph who was our office accountant standing in for our VP / Comptroller, Raymond Stroud who was absent from work that day.

My administrative assistant, Kim Burgess, was in her small workspace adjacent to mine ready to pop up around the corner and aid me if I needed anything for that meeting making it a total of eight employees who joined me in that area.

We started the meeting and completed discussing one item. Since I had to read the notes off of my computer, I leaned back in my leather chair to glance at the next item on the agenda, and before I could look back up, at 9:02am, a tornado-like concussive force hurled me away from my desk and flung me against the wall like spaghetti in a toddler's hand.

The noise was deafening.

When I came to my senses, I was surrounded by boulders and twisted wires. A cement pillar smashed my chair, and a large steel beam rolled on the floor beside me. Concrete dust and smoke blurred my vision, but I could see daylight where my office ceiling used to be. It smelled as if the building was on fire.

I thought my desk was gone, but it was hanging over the edge of what was left of the floor. The walls and ceilings had disappeared. My employees had vanished. Where had they gone? Why did they leave me here?

There was a brief moment of extremely unsettling and eerie silence. "What on earth is happening?" I wondered. The only thing I could hear were office papers fluttering through the air.

I eventually untangled myself and got to my feet. Once I could see through the concrete dust, I realized that what appeared to be half of the building was gone. It was very disorienting, and I still did not realize at the moment that my employees had been hurled below to their deaths with the remaining floors pancaked on top of them. I was as confused as I had ever been, but my survival instincts kicked in, and I knew one thing.

The decimated Alfred P. Murrah Building minutes after the Oklahoma City Bombing on April 19, 1995.

I needed OUT.

I yelled for help, and soon the air was filled with cries for help from other victims as well.

However, two distinct voices rang out to me, and I'll never forget them as they were two men from the General Services

Administration (GSA) who recognized me: John Crisswell and Rick Garringer.

"Florence, is that you?!" they yelled.

I confirmed it was, and they told me to get as close to the edge of the cliff as possible, hang over, reach high, and they would grab me by the wrists to pull me up, so I did just that, and they led me out of the building.

Bombing Memories – Blood and Prayers on the Plaza[1]

Once I was outside on the plaza, as I was experiencing some shock and anxiety over my staff who had been in the room with me who had all disappeared right before my eyes, I was so cold and scared.

I had experienced a small cut on one of my hands, and I had been tapping my forehead and some blood had streamed down my face making it look like I was more injured than I actually was (at least at that early stage).

I saw several walking wounded people. There was blood everywhere, and glass had maimed a number of them.

---

[1] See "Bombing Memories – Byron Russell, The Man Who 'Found' Me" p. 34

However, it was when I witnessed some firefighter's retrieving small, limp, bloodied, bodies from the daycare area that I began to really panic.

There is nothing more awful to see than a dead child, and what was worse was my personal connection to them. I really did not want to compute in my mind that those were the same precious little ones that I would see playing outside my window on a daily basis. An unexplainable feeling of "*This is very real and very awful*" washed over me upon such a horrible sight.

I began to panic as the unknown fate of my employees started to race through my mind. Simultaneously, one of the first people that I recognized on the plaza was a young man, Steve Rogers, whom I had had the privilege of calling my step-son for many years when I was married to his father. His father worked in the Murrah Building also, and he was there looking for both of us.

Steve was working in the federal court house nearby for the United States Courts Division. We hugged and hugged and very soon they made the entire crowd move further away from the Plaza as the first responders and authorities began to arrive.

Steve and I went to the street on the south side of the original U.S. Post Office Building on Northwest 3rd Street close to the Federal Reserve Bank.

I was trembling from the chill in the air and the shock that I was experiencing.

Steve told me to stay put where we had been standing and that he was going to go inside to his office and get his jacket to wrap around me.

Before Steve could leave to go inside, a young man suddenly appeared beside us and was trying to find out how I was as he could tell from my bloody face that I had been in the Murrah Building.

Soon, Steve asked him if he would stay with me while he went inside to get his jacket.

Seeing my trauma, after Steve had left, the young man hugged me close and said: "Why don't we just say a prayer." He said such a great little prayer that was such a comfort at the time, but I have never been able to remember his words again.

Steve soon returned and told us that they wouldn't let him go inside the building to get his jacket.

The young man left us. I often referred to him in some of my early speeches as an angel that appeared from nowhere and then disappeared. I was anxious to get back to the plaza area to see if I could find any of my employees, and I did find a few of them, some with serious injuries, sitting on the streets among the dozens of others that were streaming out of the building rubble with blood everywhere and screaming for help.

I had been looking for my son, Terry, whom I knew was there somewhere looking for me, but I hadn't found him, and I needed to go to the bathroom really bad by that time, so I left the scene and found myself stumbling into the close by Catholic Church rectory that looked empty but so badly damaged. I went downstairs into the lower floor and found a bathroom. The entire place was scattered with the beautiful pieces of china and dishes and so much damage everywhere. I didn't see anyone in the church and left very quickly.

When I left the church and tried to return to the plaza area where the injured were being brought, there was a warning for everyone to evacuate the area as they suspected another bomb.

There was a medical bus driving around the area and taking some of the injured to hospitals and also to a triage station that had been set up at the nearby civic center.

Someone insisted that I get on the bus. I did that, but I became more anxious as we kept driving around, so as soon as the bus stopped at the triage station, I got off. I decided I was feeling no pain and didn't even think about going to a hospital. I wanted to find the rest of my employees.

Where were they? Were they hurt? I needed to see them. Later, I would discover that I had indeed needed a hospital, but the adrenaline in my body prevented me from feeling any pain.

While at the triage station, I told one of the nurses that I had not been able to let my sons know that I had made it out of the building and had no serious injuries. The nurse could tell I was in a panic to contact them. She told me that if I felt like walking, I should go to a nearby apartment complex where she lived and tell them to let me come in and use their phone.

About that time, I saw two of my young male tellers who had made it out of the building.

Neither seemed too terribly injured, but I did notice that one was without his shoes. They were both excited to see me alive and ended up walking with me to the apartment complex where they left me.

I was grateful to add them to the handful of healthy employees I had seen since the explosion, and it briefly provided some reprieve from the overwhelming anxiety I was experiencing.

I went inside the apartment lobby and begged the lobby receptionist to use the phone so I could call my son, Terry. My mind was so scrambled that the only telephone number I could recall was of the little Coffee Cup Café in my hometown where my sister, Joellyn, worked.

Strangely enough, Joellyn's daughter, Tammy, had called her earlier that day as she watched the tragedy unfold on the television. She had already given Terry's pager number to Joellyn to try to reach us since she knew that Terry and I worked downtown. My sister was so glad and relieved to hear my voice. She told me the entire town had just stopped to watch their televisions, and she gave me Terry's pager number.

The receptionist dialed Terry's pager number for me, and that was ultimately how I reached him.

Bombing Memories - My Son, Terry's, Bombing Day Experience

As I've mentioned youngest son, Terry L. Rose, was working as a marketing consultant for Oklahoma Natural Gas at the time of the bombing. I want you to read his bombing day experience in his own words. Our "bombing day stories" merge when I reached him on his pager.

My day began in prayer as I attended the Mayor's prayer breakfast at the Myriad Convention Center. When I arrived at my office, it seemed like a normal day at work at Oklahoma Natural Gas. I was just filling my coffee cup for the second time, and one of my co-workers was walking toward me. I will never forget the look on her face when our building began to shake. The sound was terrifying to say nothing of the shock wave that hit the building. In an instant, we knew something on a major scale of destruction had occurred.

The first questions everyone had were: "What happened, and where did it occur?" When I saw the large cloud of black smoke billowing from the north, I immediately thought of the Alfred P. Murrah Federal Building where my mother, Florence Rogers worked on the third floor as the CEO of the Federal Employees Credit Union.

The entire north side of the majestic Murrah Building was made of large glass windows so that people on each of the nine floors could view the surrounding downtown area. Those beautiful reflective windows could be seen at a distance, so when I ran to look out of our office window and saw no windows in the Murrah Building, I knew this was a horrible sign. Then, I heard a co-worker, Stan Tucker, yelling, "Let's evacuate, immediately!"

Within two minutes, I was climbing the stairs of the plaza and on its roof. The plaza housed the parking garage for employees and visitors of the Murrah Building, so it was nearby enough that I could see blue sky all the way through the building where its powerful edifice had once been-- especially toward the east end where my mother's office was located.

I ran toward the building with the sole thought of my mother's fate. An entire section of the building was just gone. Was she okay? Was she even alive? Before reaching the Murrah Building, I ran to the Federal Courthouse Building, and the guard recognized me: "Terry, it was a bomb...it was a bomb," he said.

A bomb?!

In natural gas-rich Oklahoma, we had imagined an accidental explosion, but ***a bomb?!*** *In Oklahoma City?! Who in the world would light a bomb,* or—more scarily—who in the world would light a bomb ***among us?!***

Panic had really started to set in as the reality hit me. Again, I found myself running down the street. As I ran, my panic turned into terror the closer I got to the Murrah Building.

There were injured and bleeding people everywhere. The emergency vehicles were starting to arrive, and the sounds of police, fire, and ambulance sirens filled the air. It was then that we were shoved from the scene by a rescue worker and told to clear the area.

As I made my way from the scene in the streets, I saw many of my Oklahoma Natural Gas Company family standing on the corner. I explained that my mother was on the third floor of the building, and, at that point, I could not hold back the tears of fright any longer. All of my co-workers instantly came to my emotional rescue. They each offered warm thoughts of reassurance and displays of true friendship. Suddenly, I knew that I had to be strong. My faith in God was never more evident to me.

A great peace began to find its way into my soul, and I knew one of two things were to happen in my life that day. Either I would hold my mother in my arms, or I would have to give her to God, so He could hold her in His. This was my strength.

Then, I heard my name being yelled.

Jerry Bowers, a heating and air conditioning contractor that I had worked with for several years, was running toward me.

His wife, Carol, whom everyone called Carrie, also worked in the Murrah Building but on the first floor for the Social Security Administration.

Jerry and I held on to one another as though we were brothers, united by the common bond of loss and hope.

As we embraced, the authorities announce the threat of a second bomb, and the police and first responders moved all of us to NW 10th Street.

There was utter chaos. Most people bolted from the scene, terrified and wrought with fear at the possibility of yet another explosion.

Others continued to run toward the building screaming the names of their loved ones who might have been stuck in the rubble and would now surely perish even if they had survived the first bomb. First responders were also fleeing the site, but a number of them refused to leave as they were mid-rescue and could not bear the thought of abandoning a terrified victim stuck in the rubble and left to die.

Jerry and I fled to the basement of St. Anthony Hospital where the list of names was being written on the wall as the injured were brought in. The list was growing steadily as we watched. Every time the nurses added a name, Jerry and I would run to the wall and search diligently for our loved one.

At 12:34 p.m., three hours and thirty two minutes after the devastating blast, my pager sounded. It was a downtown number that I didn't recognize. My heart beat fast as I dialed the number.

A kind voice answered and put me on hold. Those brief seconds seemed like an eternity.

Turns out that voice belonged to the sweet lady in the apartment complex lobby who had dialed my pager for my anxious mother.

Suddenly, I heard the voice that had awakened me so many mornings when I was a child.

It was Mom. I fell into a chair and sobbed.

Mom's injuries included some superficial lacerations on her legs, a minor blow to her head, and a deep bruise on her lower hip at the base of her spine.

My car was locked in a parking lot—guarded by a National Guard member, so my wife, Ginna's father took mom and I to Mom's physician's office, where Mom was seen very quickly by her family doctor.

Mom's doctor was amazed that she was in such good condition, considering what she had just lived through.

Later, we discovered that she would require neck surgery, but the fact that she was alive at all was a miracle—let alone mentally coherent with seemingly no debilitating injuries.

Mom had been silent all of the way from downtown to her driveway.

Once we arrived at her home around 2pm that afternoon, Mom's neighbor, Virginia, was waiting for her.

She wrapped Mom in a big hug.

As Virginia held her, Mom began to weep, but then, just as suddenly as the tears had begun, Mom dried them and said she "had work to do."

Not long before the bombing, after some issues with ice storms, the credit union had compiled an employee contact list in case of inclement weather so that the leadership could notify everyone whether or not to come to work.

That turned out to be quite handy because I took that list and went to her next door neighbor and began calling employees' families.

She was busy with her home telephone doing the same thing. We were able to account for 13 of her staff that were either not at work that day or had escaped.

There were still 18 missing. (There were 33 total employees including my mother, and one of them was a part-time employee who wasn't at work that day.)

We relayed this information to the FBI and the Oklahoma State Bureau of Investigation.

By evening's fall, we had begun to check again the credit union employee list and had made several calls to apartment complex managers asking for help in checking on children and pets that might have been home alone and needed assistance. Everyone was so willing to do whatever we requested.

I attended six funerals the following week. We buried Jerry's wife Carol, on Tuesday. Again at the sight of me, Jerry and I embraced and shared the common bond that was developed that day, April 19th, 1995 at a terribly tragic event in Oklahoma City.

Bombing Memories – Johnny Wade

The explosion had gone off, and I had just freed myself from the office rubble. There I was. Standing in the most eerie silence I had ever heard; and haven't heard a more eerie silence in the decades since.

My seven employees who had been meeting with me in my office had vanished, and the silence was broken only by the sound of falling papers fluttering through the air.

I stood there confused and somewhat disoriented, but then quickly moving into survival mode and contemplating how could I get out on the cement ledge just under my office and then maybe jump down onto the plaza.

As I stood there, I suddenly heard someone groaning, gasping for air, and trying desperately to holler for help. I looked to my left where the credit unions collections office and comptroller's offices were. Hanging halfway out of the window was a man covered with dust and debris and bleeding very badly from his nose and mouth.

"Hang on. Someone will be here soon to get you help," I managed to get out.

I did not know who this person was, but as I observed his dark gray shirt, slight graying hair, and that he was covered with debris, I concluded that he might be one of the building maintenance employees, or had perhaps been working for one of the contractors remodeling space in the building.

Seeing a person as badly injured as this gentleman was a jarring experience. I repeatedly spoke of it with my sister, and she would always follow up with: "Did you found out who he was yet?" I hadn't, and it haunted me for weeks.

A few months after the bombing, I was invited to attend the Annual Federal Employees Recognition Luncheon where federal employees who had earned outstanding recognition were honored each year. I didn't see many faces that I knew, so I chose to sit at a table with some of the U.S. Courts employees whom I had met a few times.

As the names of the honorees were called, I heard the host mention that they were posthumously honoring Johnny Wade, an employee of the Federal Highway Administration (FHA) who had perished in the Oklahoma City Bombing. Johnny's widow accepted the award on his behalf. I picked up the program to view the photos of the award recipients. Sure enough, Johnny Wade was the man I had seen on the ledge next to mine.

It was then I realized that he had died that day. I dug in my purse, tore off a deposit slip from my checkbook, and started writing a note to his widow who had been sitting nearby the table where I was sitting.

My note explained that I was probably the last one who saw Johnny alive and that I would like to speak with her when or if she should ever want to talk to me. I scribbled my home phone number and slipped her the note as everyone was leaving.

Many days passed, and late one night, my home telephone rang.

The voice on the other end of the phone said: “My name is Joannie Wade, and I’m not really sure that I want to talk to you, Florence, but for some reason, I do, and I want to ask you what makes you sure that the man you saw was my husband.”

She then asked me questions such as: “What color shirt did this man have on?” and “Was his hair sprinkled with gray?” I verified her questions with the correct answers. She then asked me what kind of injuries I thought he had. I told her what I thought they possibly were, and she verified the injuries that ended Johnny’s life that day.

This was one of the tensest and saddest calls I have ever participated in. The conversation ended with Joannie promising to visit the credit union and meet me in person. She did, and we became close through the months ahead.

We made sure to connect with each other whenever the subsequent anniversaries have rolled around every April 19th.

As sad as his death is, I was so relieved to not only solve the mystery of *“who the man on the ledge was,”* but to learn who *Johnny Wade* was: a hard-working husband, father, and servant to the United States government.

Bombing Memories – Byron Russell, The Man Who "Found" Me

In the years immediately following the bombing—I fulfilled several speaking requests around the globe, and I was in particularly high demand from credit union organizations.

I was starting to wonder if everyone was getting tired of hearing my story. Looking back, that doesn't really make sense.

Yes, I was the one who was repeating the story over and over, but to the various audiences, it was their first time hearing it. Nonetheless, I was "inside my own head a bit" and wondered if I might need to stop accepting so many speaking invites.

Then, I was invited to a program sponsored by Crossings Community Church, where the keynote speaker was a Holocaust survivor, and something compelled me to attend. I was among a handful of Murrah survivors who were introduced on the stage, but I was far more interested in listening to the Holocaust survivor.

When the speaker finished, I went up front, introduced myself and told her that I would like to know when a person realizes the time to quit telling their story.

Her answer was: "As long as you are touching lives, just keep telling your story." That answer is why I kept telling my story for several years and still fulfill requests decades later.

As I made my way back to a seat, a young man approached me and told me that he was so glad and exited to see me. I asked him who he was, and he said: "My name is Byron Russell. I'm the one who found you on the street in front of the Federal Reserve Bank. We prayed together."

My angel!

How excited I was to meet him at last! I told Byron how often I had thought of him through the years and how many times I spoke of "the angel who had appeared from somewhere, held me, and said a prayer over me" on that very dark day in Oklahoma City. Byron told me that he was living in Edmond. He wrote a little note with his address and phone number on the event program.

I still have that little note.

Bombing Memories – Pantyhose

My sons did not learn that I had survived the bombing until nearly noon that day.

When Terry finally found me, we had to walk to the perimeter of the cordoned off area which had been established by the Oklahoma National Guard. We met his father-in-law who had driven to pick us up and was on the outskirts of the safety zone. He took me immediately to my family doctor to make sure I was okay. I had a terribly bruised bottom, a few small bruises here and there, and a few cuts down my left leg where the glass had taken chunks of skin out.

By the time I got to the doctor's office, my panty hose had sealed off the cuts, and when I removed them so my doctor could see if I needed stitches, some of the places began to bleed and make a puddle on the floor.

I threw the panty hose in his trash, but I did notice that there were no up and down runners that the panty hose company had raved about their hose in the marketing. There were only the holes. My doctor gave me a tetanus shot and a prescription for pain and a sleep aid and I went home.

Several weeks went by, and one evening in my mailbox was a pretty stern letter from the panty hose company telling me that I owed for the last shipment and that I was going to be turned into a collection agency if not paid immediately.

My days had been long ones since the bombing, and like so many others affected by that event, mortgage payments, bill payments, etc. were not the first priority any longer. Late one night after I got home, I sat down and wrote them a long letter telling them why I had neglected to pay the bill and sent them a check. I also mentioned that they were correct in their marketing, that they had no runs in them, only the holes.

About ten days later, I received a notice in my mailbox that I had a package at the post office in Moore about 15 minutes south of Oklahoma City. I had been going to work about 6am every morning for weeks, so one morning soon after receiving that notice, I called the office and told my sole surviving Vice President, Raymond Stroud, that I would be late so that I could retrieve my mail.

The package at the post office was a huge box from the panty hose company containing dozens of hose with a very sweet letter explaining that they "had watched the Oklahoma City tragedy on their television screens" and that they just felt like they had to send me something. They sent me so many pairs that I didn't have to buy pantyhose for 10 years, and by then no one was wearing the things anymore!

Bombing Memories – The Dress

As far as my attire went, I walked away from that bombing site with only a tear my dress, while some people's clothing was literally blown off of them. The dress is now on display at the Oklahoma City National Memorial & Museum.

Bombing Memories - The Shady Preacher

Credit Unions from around the world including Canada, and Australia immediately began sending donations to the various funds to assist with the families and survivors of Federal Employees Credit Union. Several of the women at the credit union were the sole breadwinners in their respective families. Fourteen little children belonged to those employees of the credit union that were killed.

We soon realized that many of the families were going to need funds for funerals and living expenses before any insurance benefits were received.

Those funds soon reached 1.6million dollars and a special committee was established at the Oklahoma Credit Union League in Tulsa to determine the purpose and distribution of those funds. They knew the survivors of the credit union, including me, would be busy with the business of re-establishing the credit union and looking for a permanent location. I was so grateful for that assistance since I was dealing with grieving survivors, family members, insurance business and the list was lengthy.

We opened accounts at the credit union in order to allocate funds for the education of the children left without their mothers.

The employees that had been killed had life insurance benefits as well as a benefit from Federal Workers Comp. Any loans they had at the credit union were paid off immediately by the insurance carrier (CUNA Mutual), and beneficiaries were paid for any accrued annual leave benefits plus Social Security. Each family account soon had significant balances for their future needs and were made available immediately.

I was somewhat taken aback one day to receive a call from an investment firm stating that they would be investing most of the children's funds from one of the employees that had died. Then they stated that the minister of that family would be coming by for 10% of the amount in the account and for me to have the checks ready. I can safely say that this request made me somewhat angry which is not my personality. I was even more angry when the minister showed up for his check driving a Jaguar automobile. This day was not so good for me as I wrote those checks because

I knew the needs of that little family and had never dreamed that the churches would expect anything from that horrible event that affected so many.

The education funds that were established for ALL of the children of those killed in the bombing were held in trust, and many of them will never have to worry about that expense in their future lives.

McVeigh's Bomb – Why He Said He Did It

My friend, Major Chris Fields, is most known as the fireman in the famous photo, holding a deceased one- year-old girl, Baylee Almon. It became known as "the face of the Oklahoma City Bombing.

In Chris' book, Out of Chaos, he states that he doesn't like the phrase "Oklahoma City Bombing" because that bomb didn't belong to us, and neither did it come from us. I tend to agree and use the phrase simply for reference since that is what it came to be known as worldwide."

America's most notorious domestic terrorist, Timothy McVeigh, built an explosive that included approximately fifteen 55-gallon barrels of ammonium nitrate fertilizer mixed with diesel fuel oil and laced with blasting caps and dynamite. This troubled young man who was young enough to be my son intended to do some real damage.

McVeigh co-conspired with Michael Fortier and Terry Nichols, former army buddies with whom he had bonded over an awful book titled The Turner Diaries. The book, which contains a fictional account of an uprising against an oppressive government culminating in a truck-bombing of the FBI headquarters, served as McVeigh's blueprint for the murderous Oklahoma City blast.

I am purposely not giving a lot of attention to the "why" inside of McVeigh's twisted psyche, but for educational purposes, the readers should know that over time, McVeigh became very disgruntled with the American government for various reasons including disillusionment with the military after his service in The Gulf War and a deep frustration with the government's handling of the following incidents:

1. 1992 Ruby Ridge standoff with former Green Beret, Randy Weaver, in Idaho

2. 1993 Waco, Texas standoff with the David Koresh-led Branch Davidians.

In fact, McVeigh was one of several protesters of what he felt was excessive government overreach and intervention in Waco. On the final day of the deadly standoff, April 19, 1993, when over 70 people perished in the compound raid including a number of children under the age of 16, a fuse went off in McVeigh's mind. He selected that exact anniversary date, two years later`—April 19, 1995--to enact his "revenge" on the American federal government by attacking a bastion of the government, the majestic, nine-floor Alfred P. Murrah Building, in downtown Oklahoma City which housed a number of federal agencies as well as a daycare full of children on the second floor.

McVeigh's Bomb – My Testimony At The Trial

Timothy McVeigh was convicted of mass murder on June 2, 1997, and I was one of the survivors who testified at both his and his co-conspirator, Terry Nichols', separate trials which were both held in Denver Colorado.

There were some who attended the trials as spectators, but I never did that. Between my own survival and the constant barrage of media coverage and interviews, I had enough "reliving" of that fateful day and did not need yet another avenue for rehashing its horror. I spent as little time there as possible.

Once, during the trial, I went up on a Sunday and was to testify on Monday. At noon that day, they told me that my testimony would be better the following week and asked if I would "mind terribly" coming back then. They were very cognizant of my feelings about spending time in Denver, so I knew they would not have asked me to sacrifice if it weren't necessary. I told them that we were all on the same side and that they "knew better than me when my testimony would work best."

There was one "bright spot" about going to Denver, and that was my opportunity to visit with many of my friends and credit union members who had been assigned to the trials. Several of them included me in their get-togethers at the end of those long days at their respective hotel lobbies. This also opened the door for me to make several new friends who were taking care of the witnesses and their family members.

I had several meetings and "practice runs / prep sessions" with the prosecuting legal team before I actually testified. Each time I traveled to the meeting site, my adrenaline flowed at a very high level. The security was so rigid, and it was such a sight! I had a very high level of anxiety, but it got a bit easier with each trip, and I grew as accustomed as I could to that tense environment.

I will never forget the night before the first day when I was to finally testify.

Late one evening, I met with the lead prosecuting attorney, Joe Hartzler, who had been the Assistant United States Attorney of the Central District of Illinois. Then Attorney General Janet Reno and Patrick Ryan, the United States Attorney for the Western District of Oklahoma at the time, had announced him for this position. A young man in his early 40's, this was a huge undertaking for Mr. Hartzler.

As Mr. Hartzler and his team explained to me some of the procedures that would take place in the courtroom, I retrieved some notes from my briefcase and placed them in front of me. They began to show me the photos of the staff I had lost, and I was to identify each one, tell what their title was at the credit union, and how long they had worked for me. I started to look at my notes that contained information about each employee's tenure at the FECU when, suddenly, Mr. Hartzler slapped the table with a loud crack and told me that I could not use notes in the courtroom. "Would you

please know by morning the information without using notes?!"

Whoa. I was a 60+ year-old woman. How old was I when someone last slapped a table at me? Had my parents ever even done that before?

"Yes, sir. I can."

As you can imagine, I did not sleep all night long. Thank goodness for the adrenaline! I kept reviewing the names, titles, and tenures of my employees over and over and over again. I knew them perfectly at the trial the next day, and that information is still permanently embedded in my memory bank.

As I took the witness stand, I found myself watching Mr. Hartzler's facial expressions to see if I could gauge how well I was or wasn't doing. Only about six faces materialized for me in the courtroom that day. All the rest were just a blur to me.

I had participated in many courtroom settings during my career as the CEO of the FECU, but I had never participated in a federal trial. On slow days, I had observed some federal courtroom proceedings when our credit union offices were on the same floor as the U.S. Attorney's offices...BUT until I was actually on that witness stand myself, I had no clue how nervous I could actually get in that situation.

When I was done, the attorneys told me I did a good job, so I was pleased about that.

I was treated with the utmost respect and met with such caring attitudes by the court personnel during all of my court appearances in the Denver federal trials and also during the state trials in McAlester, Oklahoma. Even when McVeigh's defense attorneys questioned me, they showed great compassion towards me. I appreciated that, and it made those court experiences much easier.

I once felt some hostility towards McVeigh's legal defense team. How could anyone take on a case like this? However, the irony of all of this is that as angry as McVeigh was at our government, it was that very same government that afforded him with a fair trial. Even mass murderers deserve representation in the United States legal system.

McVeigh's bomb in Oklahoma City still stands as the largest act of domestic terrorism in United States history, and I pray this is never exceeded. McVeigh was ultimately sentenced to death and died of lethal injection on June 11, 2001 just months prior to the September 11th attacks which became the largest foreign terrorist attack on American soil.

Eerie Irony

Jerry Rose, my oldest son, now lives in Jacksonville, Florida. (Jerry and his younger brother Terry's father was my first husband Dean. I speak more about my personal life in Chapter 5.)

At the time of the bombing, Jerry was living in Perry, Oklahoma. He and his wife, Barbara, were working for Ditch Witch/Charles Machine Works, a Perry-based manufacturer of underground construction machines.

As I mentioned earlier, Terry, was working downtown. Terry communicated with his brother and discouraged Jerry and Barbara to get on the highway that day until they learned my fate due to the chaos.

Jerry and Barbara told me that the entire plant at Ditch Witch shut down, and everyone stood around the television to watch the tragedy unfold on the office television screens while comforting them because they told their co-workers that I worked in the building.

Once I was found, Jerry and Barbara came to Oklahoma City as soon as they knew I was okay and stayed late into the night.

Time passed, and one day, Jerry called me from his desk at work and said: “Mom, I have been thinking about everything, and this is really ironic:

1. I was the only resident in Perry that had a family member in the Murrah Building.
2. Timothy McVeigh was arrested in Perry where I live.
3. He rented the Ryder Truck in Junction City, KS where I was born.
4. They incarcerated McVeigh at Florence, Colorado.”

About two years ago, I called Jerry and told him there was another irony that he could add to his story. He said: “What’s that, Mom?” I then told him that the Memorial is now growing seedlings from the survivor tree in Jacksonville, Florida where he now lives.

The Rebuild - Damage Caused by the Bombing

Losing 18 of my 33 employees in the bombing was a devastating hit. On top of which, I lost both a credit committee member and a board of directors member.

Not only did I suffer emotional shock, but I was hit in the face with the stark reality of attempting to rebuild a financial institution that was very important to so many.

Of the 15 credit union employees who survived, five were hospitalized.

Five walked out. Five were not at the office that day.

One of our credit union committee members, Dianne Dooley, was also hospitalized.

Hospitalized

1. Patti Hall – VISA Clerk
2. Amy Petty (Downs) – VISA Clerk
3. Terri Shaw (Talley) – Financial Services Clerk
4. Enetrice Smiley – Teller
5. Ellen Young – Accounting Clerk

Exited The Building

1. Florence Rogers
2. Joe May
3. Bobbi Purvine
4. Jason Williamson
5. Mary Schonberger

Absent From The Office

1. Brad Grant
2. Lisa Johnson
3. Jennifer Boone
4. Kimberley Ritchie
5. Pam Cavazos

The Rebuild – A Reporter's Surprise (Unveiling my bruised full moon!)

In Chapter 3, I go into some detail about the inner-office professional challenges I endured to get the credit union back on its feet, so I won't delve too far into those details in this section. However, I want to share this one particularly humorous story about those challenges.

On April 22, 1995, three days after the bombing, I hobbled to the location where our credit union had just reopened the day prior—only 48 hours after the tragedy. There, I was to meet Carol Anne Burger, reporter for the Credit Union Times Magazine who had flown to Oklahoma City soon after the bombing to cover the story.

A young lady reporter from the Wall Street Journal had been in OKC to cover a different assignment and was told to stay over to cover the bombing that had happened on Wednesday. Those two reporters requested an interview, and I showed up to visit with them.

We were in a large conference room at the Tinker Federal Credit Union location. After we chatted a bit, they asked me about any injuries I had suffered from the bombing. I told them that at my age, I didn't have many inhibitions, and proceeded to lower my very loose slacks I was wearing that day to expose my very, very bruised behind that was all black and blue from my landing on the floor where the bomb had landed me.

When I turned around to show my injury, I felt a camera flash. Sure enough, Carol had taken a quick photo. I shook my finger at her and remember saying I would "get even" with her someday and that it had better stay hidden from the magazine.

Carol and I became great friends and I usually invited her to stay in my home when she was in OKC doing stories for the magazine she worked for in West Palm Beach, FL. I shared a lot of my stories with her when we found ourselves alone in my home. One was how chaotic things were at the office and how the board of directors had overplayed their roles by taking over the hiring of new staff to name one thing.

When she returned to Oklahoma in April 1996 to cover the first anniversary of the bombing, she was unpacking her luggage and shouted that she had brought me a gift. As I told her that she didn't need to bring me a gift, she unwrapped a nicely framed and professionally matted spoof replica of the front page of the CU Magazine graced with her photo of my bruised "tush." The photo was surrounded with humorous article "headlines" of the day. The date of the magazine was April Fool's Day, April 1st, 1996.

My unique professional friendship with Carol Anne was yet another relationship that was abruptly interrupted in tragedy. In 2008, Carol took her own life. This incident sent shockwaves through our office staff. She had done such a heartfelt job reporting on the progress of our credit union and had formed personal relationships with many of our employees.

The Rebuild – Hospital Visits (the full moon...again)

While my male employees emerged largely unscathed from the explosion, the women were either injured or deceased. Only one of my female employees was completely injury-free as she did not attend work that day.

I never thought that I would be visiting my employees as hospital patients—especially not several of them at the same time. As I made the rounds of hospital visits, my mind darted between the well-being of my injured employees and the employees whose bodies had not yet been recovered.

It was such an emotionally heavy time, but between getting the credit union back up and running within 48 hours and checking on my employees, I didn't take a lot of time to allow the heaviness to set in. I didn't think I could afford the time or the energy to be mentally and emotionally paralyzed by the pain.

Looking back, I wondered if this is subconsciously why I carried out the following amusement during hospital visits.

Amy Downs and Terri Talley (who still work at the credit union as I write this), were both young women in their 20s who had been severely injured in the bombing yet were conscious and able to have conversations with me.

The ladies in our office were so close with each other, so I knew that the injuries to Amy's and Terri's hearts far outweighed the injuries to their physical bodies as we all awaited news of the missing ladies' fates.

When I visited Amy's room, a priest was already there visiting her. Amy and I made some small talk, and the emotional boulder dangling above our heads was that neither her professional peers nor her mentor and supervisor, Vicky Texter, had been found among the bombed out rubble yet.

Sonja and Vicky had both been excellent employees. They were two of the seven department heads attending the meeting in my office before disappearing 3 floors below me. I loved those ladies, and I considered them friends. I was their dear Mother Goose. The thought of that heinous bombing robbing them from us and their families was unbearable.

As I inquired with Amy about her well-being and her injuries, she showed me a very nasty wound on her leg of which the bone had been exposed. I quipped: "Do you want to see my worst scar?"

Before Amy could reply, I had turned around, lifted my skirt, whipped down my pantyhose and underwear and showed her my very bruised and discolored rear-end giving the priest quite an unexpected eyeful as well.

Amy burst into a guffaw of laughter. It was a much needed moment of levity.

While I was known for having a quick wit and for not biting my tongue very much, I was not known for this type of humor. When it came to operating the credit union, I was no-nonsense and required excellence.

None of my employees would have *ever* considered a day where I was mooning them—*especially* in front of a priest.

I did the same thing with Terri Talley, but instead of a priest in the room, her family was there. I'm glad that that my antics could bring these ladies a laugh.

At least those annoying bruises were put to good use for *somebody* because the only thing they brought me was a literal pain in my rear!

The Rebuild – Never the Same

In Chapter 2, I delve into the details of my unique grieving process and a series of touching stories, but here, I want to give you a glimpse into the sudden and drastic changes that occurred in my life after the bombing. It was as if my "new normal" meant that at any moment, I was susceptible to having a new emotional experience sprung upon me without notice.

A few of those examples were directly tied to the discoveries of personal belongings found in the bombing rubble. On Meridian Avenue in Oklahoma City, a "property room" had been set up as a holding place for those belongings which was just a few blocks from our temporary office.

In one instance, one of our credit union members who had been severely injured came into my office very excited that he had just found some items in the property room where he and his wife had been sifting through things.

He came right over to my office and placed on my desk a battered photo of me and another photo of one of my deceased employees, Vicki Texter.

I am convinced that photos speak so loudly because they can help you recall even the smallest of details surrounding those moments. It's interesting which memories resurface to your mind at different times, because as he placed the items on my desk, I recalled that Vicki's photo had been taken on the same day that the television show, M.A.S.H. had ended its series run.We had decorated the offices of the credit union in M.A.S.H. style, and we had warn the costumes of our favorite characters in the series.

My life had been busy but so simple before the bombing. I realized that perhaps I had taken some things for granted.

We all do that, though, don't we? We assume that our lives will remain normal. That we'll see our co-workers the next day. That we'll go home, turn on our television, sleep, get up the next day, and repeat the cycle, but the Oklahoma City Bombing taught us that was just not the case.

No moment is guaranteed. No relationship—like the one I had with my excellent employee, Vicki Texter—is beyond a sudden interruption. Every moment should be cherished.

In another instance, shortly after we had moved into our new location around the first week of June, 1995, I was sitting at my desk and was suddenly overcome with a feeling that I cannot explain.

Tears were not far away, and the thought occurred to me that I "just had to go" to the property room and hug the GSA employee who had been assigned there. It happened to be John Crisswell, one of the two gentlemen who had helped me escape from the bombed out building.

I quickly dashed out of the office and drove as fast as I could to be with John whom I had not yet spoken with since the day of the bombing a couple of months prior. The property room was already so emotional. The news reported "numbers" of deaths, but those numbers become people when you're surrounded by their belongings.

Somehow standing there with John made it even more emotional. This man owned the hands that had pulled me from the jagged cliff of the building to safety, and now those hands where holding me as I cried with him.

I left the property room with three purses that had belonged to my staff members: two who had died and one who had been severely injured. As I describe later in chapter 2, watching spouses break into wracking sobs when they came to retrieve them were gut-wrenching moments of our shocking new reality. Purses, wallets, eyeglasses, and watches are all such personal belongings to their owners. Those purses were like remaining "pieces of them."

The Rebuild – Professionals Stepping Up to Bat For Us

As challenging as leading the rebuild was, I have to say that the credit union community stepped up to the bat like nothing most people had ever seen before.

A number of people put on their best superhero uniforms of professionalism and jumped to our rescue.

In chapter 2, I delve more into Tinker Federal Credit Union opening its facilities for us, but it's worth noting right here that under the impeccable leadership of Mike Kloiber, Tinker made it possible for the Federal Employees Credit Union to continue operating, and I would not have been able to lead the FECU rebuild process without them.

Tinker FCU had actually contacted my board of directors on the day of the bombing and offered us space in their teller training facility which was to be our location for the next 42 days. My Vice President / Comptroller, Raymond Stroud, who was absent from our office the morning of the bombing was attending a technology meeting in Florida. When he heard the terrible news of what happened to us back home, he immediately ordered new computers, had them shipped to his residence in Oklahoma City, and caught the first flight home.

My IT guy, a young man named Brad, was on reserve duty that week at nearby Fort Sill, Oklahoma. When Brad heard the news, he immediately started packing his gear to head home. He was flown to Valley Forge, PA the next day to our "hot site" location where he was to spend nearly two weeks running our computer operations from there. We flew his wife up to join him since he would not be able to attend many of the funerals of his friends and co-workers.

The Rock Island Group who stored our computer data offsite began making back-up tapes to send to the hot site and immediately began putting in phone lines and computer wiring at the Tinker Credit Union location. The Rock Island Group also put together a comprehensive document titled "A Survivor's Tale: The Rebirth of the Federal Employees Credit Union in Oklahoma City" of which excerpts are both included in this chapter.

Credit Union CEO's throughout Oklahoma City and other nearby cities were gathering to see how they could help. We had so many offers of assistance that we literally could not use everyone. We had the "luxury" (if you could even use that word in such a tragedy as this) of selecting volunteers who were using the same computer system we had been using, which really made things easier, as there was certainly no time to train anyone.

The volunteers who were sent to serve as my assistants, helped to answer the many phone calls, take notes, fend off the media, and assist with the insurance claims. I also personally instructed them to make sure I ate lunch every day, as I felt no hunger for several weeks. When I was home alone, I often skipped dinner. Therefore, I quickly dropped 15 pounds. Had those assistants not been there to force me to eat lunch, I wonder if I would eaten very much at all over those days. Sometimes, that forced lunch would be the only food I would ingest. We opened back up for business in 48 hours and 18 minutes. For 1995-level technology with no smart phones and only a fraction of the innovation we have today, I am doubly proud of the efficiency we displayed.

A SURVIVOR'S TALE

The Rebirth of the Federal Employees Credit Union in Oklahoma City

By now, you know the story. On April 19, 1995, shortly after 9:00 AM, Oklahoma City endured the most brutal terrorist attack in American history. The blast that laid waste to the Alfred P. Murrah Federal Building in downtown Oklahoma City was so intense that it shook the countryside for miles. The horrific and shocking image of the disaster seared itself into the minds of millions of Americans. Every floor of the Murrah building became a tragic story. This is the story from the third floor, where the Federal Employees Credit Union (FECU) once stood.

FECU suffered the most fearsome blow of all the businesses and agencies housed in the Federal Building. While other offices in the building were branches of larger federal organizations, such as Social Security and Veterans Administrations Services, FECU was wholly located in the destroyed structure. The seventy-five million dollar credit union served over fifteen thousand members worldwide from that office. All information technology and infrastructure, all MIS systems and telecommunications equipment, all records and all files were utterly laid to waste. Hundreds of thousands of dollars in checks, traveler's checks, and cash vanished into the smoldering rubble. The most crippling blow came to the staff -- of the thirty-three employees of the credit union, eighteen died in the blast, five were hospitalized, and many of the remaining survivors were too traumatized to return to work.

With only three of the employees of FECU and the aid of many volunteers, the credit union was open for business on Friday the 21st at 9:40 A.M., just over 48 hours after the disaster.

KEYS TO RECOVERY

The restoration of the Federal Employees Credit Union was a marvel of disaster recovery. Three factors made this possible: a sound and flexible disaster recovery strategy, the generous support of other credit unions and recovery experts, and a spot of good luck.

Though it is difficult to perceive a business which has suffered the cruel and agonizing fate that befell FECU as being "lucky," there was a genuine patch of good fortune when it came to restoring the damaged business. Amongst the survivors were CEO Florence Rogers, Vice President and Comptroller Raymond Stroud, and the FECU data processing specialist, Brad Grant. It was by dint of sheer coincidence that Grant and Stroud were both out of town at the time. Florence Rogers was in the building when the blast struck -- her survival is a miracle in and of itself. Thus, when the smoke cleared, the Credit Union had suffered an awful loss, but it did have the three key people it needed for recovery there to help restore it.

Snapshot of Page 1 of the
Rock Island Group Bombing Assessment Document

The Rebuild - Effect on our Business

It goes without saying that our rebuilding process had a profound effect on our business. A handful of our members left the credit union because they missed their favorite teller or loan officer.

Some of our members would stand in line and cry as they missed their favorite teller or loan officer. A number of our remaining staff left very soon after the bombing. Others left during the next several months. I remember begging some of them to stay because we needed their memories and knowledge of the inner workings of our office so much in the rebuilding process.

A regular "day in the life" for me might include seeing a new article pop up featuring me or one of my employees and then a new discovery of some of our office belongings. Below, are two examples.

The first example is that I remember seeing a story in Harper's Bazaar Magazine, and the photo they used of me was absolutely awful. I then noticed that our Governor's wife, Cathy Keating, who is an absolutely gorgeous woman, also looked quite terrible.

I later found out that they had purposely distorted the photos in order to make a point of how awful the tragedy was. It was some sort of reason centered around artistic expression, so I felt a bit better about it—as much as could have been expected in that type of situation. If the flawless Cathy Keating shared the awful photo layout with me, at least I wasn't alone in that odd news piece.

The second example is the recovery of money and financial records.

Our disaster was very different from a natural disaster such as a hurricane, fire, flood or earthquake, since it was a crime scene. The only disasters we had ever worried about over the years were the Oklahoma tornados or perhaps being robbed, and we hadn't worried much about that since we were located on the third floor of a Federal Building where many of the Federal law enforcement agencies offices were also located there.

Many of those Federal law enforcement agencies such as the, ATF, US Customs, U.S. Marshalls, DEA, and the Army Reserve were members of our credit union, so they took great care of any recovered items that they thought might belong to their credit union. One FBI agent brought us a roll of quarters one day that had been blown about two blocks from the bomb site. We had relocated about 12 miles from downtown. When any cash was recovered, it was turned over to our disaster recovery facility, or taken to the Federal Reserve Bank or brought directly to us.

We had received a cash shipment that very morning from the Federal Reserve Bank. I think it was $250,000. It was found in the rubble still in the cloth bags with the lead seals still in place. One of the teller's cash drawers containing her beginning cash each day of $10,000 was found early in the rescue and brought to us.

The rescuers assumed that any money that was found had to belong to the credit union since we were a financial agency.

One day I got a call from on Oklahoma City police officer who was in charge of the initial place where they had been taking a lot of the recovered items that sometimes contained cash and coins, purses and billfolds, and a lot of personal items from the desks.

He began his call: "Ms. Rogers, we've got a problem."

"What might that be Sgt. Hatfield?" I replied.

"Well, we think that some of the money that we have sent to the credit union belongs to the snack bar, the coffee cans and fruit jars from the offices that contained their coffee and flower funds, plus $37,000 that belongs to the DEA from one of their recent drug raids," he said.

Sgt. Hatfield was right, and we eventually had to give some of it back.

Apparently there was very little looting in the rescue efforts. I wondered if it was because everyone involved was just too shocked and touched by such a terrible, horrifying tragedy that had occurred in the "Bible Belt" of our nation.

My 20-year service appreciation plaque surfaced one day and it was the only item of all of my office contents that I was left with.

Very few items that were useful in the reorganization of the credit union were recovered, and some things became contaminated as the days wore on. We had to hire a de-contamination company to handle it.

One day an FBI agent called me and said that he thought he saw several small metal drawers sitting out on the plaza getting wet from the rains containing the signature cards of our members.

Sure enough, it was.

We hired some kids that summer to scan them after they were dried out. How excited we were to find those!

The Rebuild – Cheering Amid Tragedy

Any leader of any organization learns that an important role of their position is that of the "happy warrior."

No matter what challenges you face whether as small and inconvenient as an ink shortage or as large and traumatic as a mass death of employees, it is the job of the leader to maintain a positive outlook for the future.

Our demeanor—even while serious—should always be that of strength in knowing that the present inconvenience or tragedy is only temporary.

Those who follow us should read from our demeanor and hear in our words that there are better days ahead, and the dark days will eventually give way to the brighter days.

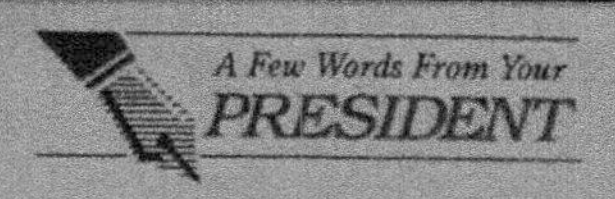

New Projects

By Florence Rogers

The past few months have been quite a challenge for the staff and officials of Federal Employees Credit Union. The hiring process is nearly complete. I feel we have hired a competent, enthusiastic staff that will carry on our legacy. Please be patient with them as they learn their roles and get acquainted with you, our member/owners.

There are many projects in the process and we have accomplished much in this short time considering all the obstacles we faced after April 19th.

Our drive through lanes are open and the members are enjoying this convenience and the Saturday hours. The downtown branch in the Old Postoffice Building on Dean A. McGee Avenue is in the beginning stages. Assignment of space had been approved, the design of the space has been done, and GSA will soon begin alterations of the space to meet our needs. We hope to be serving you before year end through this branch. In the meantime, to assist you with your financial transactions, please remember our ATM machines located in the basement of the Federal Courthouse Building and the one located in the IRS Building, the phones and the drive through lanes.

The Bethany location has proved to be very convenient to many of our members. Demographic studies shows many members living in this area and the access is easy to many others. If you haven't had an opportunity to visit this location, I invite you to do so. I think you will be pleased. Thank you for your loyalty and concerns. Your sympathy and understanding is appreciated more than words can ever express.

Florence Rogers

Florence Rogers

Concerning "Those We Lost"

In addition to 18 staff members and 2 officials of the credit union, we lost 85 other members of the credit union on April 19th.

We would like to encourage the closing of these accounts as soon as it is feasible so you will not experience tax complications for 1996. Statements on these accounts, as well as 1099's will be issued for the balance of 1995. If you have any questions or concerns, please let us know.

Many of these accounts are still being used for share draft (check) clearing and direct deposits from spouse income. We will be glad to assist you in opening these accounts on one of your own and the transfers of direct deposits. Thank you in advance. We will try to make this transition as painless as possible.

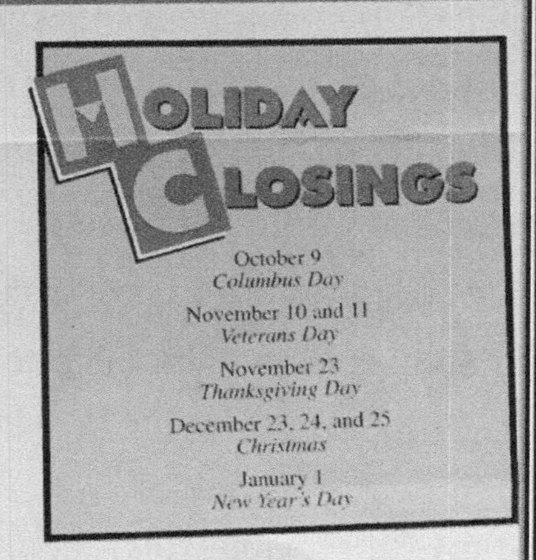

My letter in "The Federal Informer" newsletter months after the bombing.

The Rebuild - Oklahoma, We're Back!

We reopened the Federal Employees Credit Union in a brand new location on July 15, 1996 just a little over a year after the bombing, and I have to say that it was only by the grace of God and great people coming together for a purpose larger than ourselves.

If someone had said to me on the morning of April 19, 1995: *"Florence, a bomb is going to destroy your business and you're going to have to lead the rebuild of not only the actual edifice but of the morale of the company itself including hiring new employees and comforting the old ones while reassuring your clientele that everything would be back up and running smoothly."* I'm not sure what my response would have been. I've often wondered if I would have tried to hire a large task force or step down to allow someone else to take the reins, but, of course, that is not how things went at all.

Many times, God won't let us know what's ahead because he knows we'll question it or run from it. He does, however, prepare us at the exact moment that we need it.

It reminds me of the story of Moses--particularly when God called him to stand up to the pharaoh of Egypt and demand that the People of Israel be set free from bondage.

At the time, Egypt was the most powerful kingdom in the world. Moses had a litany of excuses for why he was not the one whom God should send, and God told Moses to first "Go." *Then,* He would teach Moses the words to say *(Exodus 4:12)*. God does that so often. He prepares us as we move forward—not always necessarily with a lot of heads up.

Everything happened so fast for me that I really didn't have time to run away from the situation or to ask God 20 times which direction I should go. There was no time for that! I had to jump in, and He equipped me with the strength and focus to lead even as I battled shock, grief, and the overwhelming task of steering our decimated financial institution back on track.

On July 15, 1996, by the grace of God, we reopened in a new building!

I've included copies of a number of letters of good will that I received. I hope that it blesses you to see the kindness revealed by others in the toughest of times.

Letters of Good Will List

A screenshot of most of the letters are listed below, and they are self-explanatory. However, this first letter nominating me for the National Association of State Councils on Vocational Education's Exemplary Business Involvement Award has a special story behind it, so I am providing more context with it.

For several years I have been receiving mailings concerning the National Association of State Councils on Vocational Education as well as invitations to many of their activities. I have completely ignored these mail pieces, and wondered how I might have gotten on their mailing list in the first place.

In October of 2018, some twenty three years after the bombing, I began sifting through several of my speeches and presentations as well as articles featuring my survival story that have been disseminated across the globe in preparation for this book.

In most of those pieces, I told the audiences that the credit union had 32 full time employees and a part-time high school trainee. I confess that sometimes I would not include the part-time trainee and would only mention 32 employees with eighteen of them perishing in the bombing, several seriously injured, and only seven were able to immediately return to work.

However, I now feel that I owe that precious little part-time employee a huge apology, and you will understand why I feel that way when you read that recently discovered two-page document.

Jennifer Boone was that 11th grade "little part-time employee" I referred to, and she miraculously exited the decimated building with no injuries. I now include her in the number of employees we had in the building that day bringing the total to 33 instead of 32. See the transcript of the two-page document below.

Nominating Florence Rogers for the National Association of State Councils on Vocational Education's Exemplary Business Involvement Award is going to be a "Once Upon a Time" type of adventure. It will be difficult because "Once Upon a Time" is still so current in our lives. You see, Florence Rogers is the Chief Executive Officer of Federal Employees Credit Union. If the name is still unfamiliar, Florence and the credit union she heads had a date with destiny on April 19, 1995 at 9:02 a.m. when both were the victims of the bombing of the Alfred P. Murrah Federal Building in Oklahoma City, Oklahoma.

Florence Rogers could easily have terminated participation in the Scholl-to-Work program at Eastern Oklahoma County Area Vocational Center in Choctaw, Oklahoma, and she easily could have, because of the chaos of her busy schedule and added responsibilities, returned the student apprentice to full-time school. However, the thought was not even a flicker, much less a flame. Instead, student apprentice, Jennifer Boone, was whisked into helping set up and reopen the credit union in temporary quarters and then later into new dwellings. You see, Florence realized that even though teenaged Jennifer worked only two afternoons per week, she would be experiencing vividly the loss of her work-site mentor, her co-workers and friends, and her place "to be." The trauma of such multiple separations possibly would have damaged the young worker permanently. Jennifer needed to be with the survivors in order to heal and continue living.

The impact on Jennifer has been a two-fold success-personal and professional. After a shaky, uncertain return to work, Jennifer started to feel comfortable and the grieving processes ensued. Working in the temporary offices only meant that another move and more change would be ahead—could she handle it? YES! She was needed, truly needed, and a third workday each week at the credit union was requested and approved. The experience of the bombing is difficult for an adult to comprehend and accept—for an 11th grader, comprehension and acceptance are other words for pain—the pain of people blown away—one day at work and then the next day gone forever. Tears are just a thought away.

Due to the specialness and insight of Florence Rogers and her "tending" to her flock, Jennifer's psychological growth is sound. She is completing her senior year and is now a four-day week employee. A scholarship to Rose State College will be awarded to Jennifer—and she will continue to work at Federal Employees Credit Union.

For her commitment to our youth and their education, for her commitment to the School—to-Work program, for her commitment to the feelings of a very young part-time employee, Florence Rogers, for her commitment to "rise from the ashes" like the Phoenix, we feel the choice for the NASCOVE Exemplary Business Award should be won only by our nominee—Florence Rogers!!

I really don't quite remember how the story ended with this nomination, and I don't actually know who wrote it, but I feel that the nomination alone was enough of an award. I do remember though, that Jennifer was a full time employee at the credit union when I retired in 1997—just two years after the bombing.

She worked as a teller in both of the locations when the credit union was in the process of rebuilding then moved into the headquarters building when it was finished in late 1998.

Eventually, she ended up at the downtown branch location, making less travel time for her from her home in Midwest City.

Jennifer left the credit union which is now called the Allegiance Credit Union, in December 1999 to take a position with American Fidelity Assurance in north Oklahoma City, where she continues to work as of the time that I write this.

She is happily married and the mother of a handsome son who graduated high school in May of 2019.

Jennifer and I still follow each other on social media, and I can see that she is still very close to her credit union friends with whom she shared the grieving process during the very dark days and months that followed the horrific tragedy.

Jennifer recently told me how blessed her life has been.

I'd like to think that maybe her fairly short tenure at the credit union just might have played a small part, or possibly a bigger part, in her personal and professional achievements, which have been outstanding.

Please enjoy the remainder of these precious letters which are still so dear to my heart to the day that I write this chapter.

Anonymous Hallmark letter

After the bombing, whenever one of our volunteers or team members performed an extraordinary act of customer service to customers, we "awarded" them with a "POS" merit which stood for Positively Outrageous Service.

With our members understandably shaken after the tragedy, I found the POS merits to be a positive, uplifting, and effective method for incentivizing our team amid such heavy emotional circumstances.

I have kept nearly every piece of mail that was sent to me during this time including the following letter, but I have no idea to this day who it is from. Their words were kind, however and I cherish the letter to this day.

Florence,

This is my own personal POS to you. I believe that's what FECU calls them. I could not sleep last night, and, for some reason, you were heavy on my heart.

I think you deserve the biggest POS of all. I think you are the most incredible lady I have ever known. Not only did you survive this horrible tragedy, you came back with such a wonderful positive attitude.

You truly have made FECU a fully functional credit union again. You have made myself and all of my other new coworkers feel like we are a part of what is left of the FECU family.

I am so sorry for the loss of your employees. I just want to commend you for picking up the pieces, holding your head up high, and marching on.

Thank you so much for the opportunity to work for you and your FECU family. It's really not important who I am. I t was important that you be recognized for your extraordinary inner strength.

Please don't ever forget how much God loves you.

Thinking of you card from my friend, Kay

I received numerous "thinking of you" cards with simple messages from people letting me know that I was on their minds.

These small gestures and simple words played a large part in helping me through such a challenging time.

Philippians 1:3 "I thank my God upon every remembrance of you..."

To know you is to like you,
Because it's really true—
Life is a little brighter,
When I think of you!

With love,
Kay

Mike Kitchen letter from CUNA Mutual Insurance Group, April 28, 1995

Dear Ms. Rogers,

On behalf of CUNA Mutual Group, I wish to express our sincere respects to you and your family. Our first concern is for your speedy recovery.

Your file will be handled promptly, confidentially, and in a caring manner.

We will keep you updated and will assist you in whatever capacity you require.

Our role is to provide you with support, information, and appropriate referrals for you and your family during this difficult time. During the next several days, our claims staff representative will contact you to explain your benefits and to help you secure them.

Sincerely,
Michael B. Kitchen

President
Chief Executive Officer

Mike Kitchen letter from CUNA Mutual Insurance Group, June 16, 1995

Dear Florence,

It was my privilege and pleasure to meet with you at the Credit Union Executives Society Convention.

Also, I want you to know how impressed I was with your presentation to the delegates.

I'm looking forward to seeing you again at the Oklahoma League Annual Meeting.

Sincerely,
Michael B. Kitchen
President
Chief Executive Officer

Robert "Bob" V. Bianchini letter from Oklahoma Credit Union League and Credit Union Foundation, June 20, 1995

Dear Florence:

On behalf of the worldwide credit union community, we want to extend our deepest sympathies for the loss of your credit union colleagues and the personal trauma you experienced, and offer a helping hand during the is difficult time.

As you may know, since April 19th, contributions have been sent in from all over the world to help you and others hurt by the bombing.

Credit Union Foundation, Inc. has asked us to help distribute these contributions in a fair and timely manner in the hope that they will be of some assistance in your time of sorrow and recovery.

Enclosed is a check for $5,000 from Credit Union Foundation, Inc. to help with any immediate financial needs you may have. Plans are underway for additional distributions, and you will be receiving more information in that regard in the near future.

Also, you can expect to receive a phone call from Mary Cunningham to answer any questions you might have.

Our thoughts and prayers are with you, as are those of credit union people across the country and throughout the world.

Sincerely,
Robert V. Bianchini
President/CEO

Patricia A. Brownell letter from Credit Union Foundation, July 10, 1995

Dear Ms. Rogers,

On June 20th, a check was sent to you to help with immediate financial needs you and your family may have had as a result of the April 19th disaster. We now enclose an additional distribution in the amount of $16,528.38.

Our deepest sympathies are with you during this difficult time.

Best regards,

Patricia Brownell
Executive Director

CC: Robert Bianchini

David A. Miller National Association of Federally-Insured Credit Unions (NAFCU) letter, July 14, 1995

Dear Ms. Rogers,

On behalf of the credit union community, please accept the enclosed check as an expression of our deepest sympathy to the loss of family and friends. Although, there are no words that we can say which would ease the pain and sorrow, other than we are here to help in any way that we can.

Over the last few months, we have received hundreds of letters from the credit union community in support of the effort to provide aid to the victims and families of the Federal Employees Credit Union.

This level of response from the credit unions during this time of tragedy, truly demonstrates the basic philosophy of "people helping people."

David A. Miller
NAFCU Foundation Chair

Wayne Benson letter from CUNA Mutual Group, July 14, 1995

Dear Florence:

I was honored to have the opportunity to meet you at the Southeast Regional Volunteers Conference.

Your presentation on disaster recovery was excellent.

The message was very powerful and clearly depicts the true spirit of the Credit Union Movement.

Your staff and their families will continue to be in our thoughts and prayers as recovery from the bombing continues.

Florence, you showed me a newsletter which honored your deceased employees.

If you have an extra copy you could spare, I would appreciate receiving one.

Hope to see you in the near future.

Sincerely,
Wayne Benson, CLU ChFC
Senior Marketing Officer

Patricia A. Brownell letter from Credit Union Foundation, October 16, 1995

Dear Florence,

On June 20th, a check was sent to you to help with immediate financial needs you and your family may have had as a result of the April 19th disaster. On July 10th, an additional distribution was made to you in the amount of $16,528.38. We now enclose the third and final distribution in the amount of $5,253.24.

On behalf of the credit union movement, we wish you and your family the best.

Sincerely,

Patricia A. Brownell
Executive Director
CC: Robert Bianchini

Patricia A. Brownell letter to Brian Hansen re: custodial account from Credit Union Foundation, October 17, 1995

This letter is special. It concerns Brian Hansen, whose mother, Claudine Ritter, was killed in the bombing, six months prior. Brian had celebrated his 18th birthday just prior to the bombing, so we had to fight for him to receive his benefits. Claudine was a single mother.

Dear Brian:

On August 7, 1995, a wire transfer was sent to the Brian Hansen Custodial Account in the name of Florence Rogers. A final distribution of $10, 506.48 will be made by wire transfer on October 18, 1995 to this account.

On behalf of the credit union movement, we wish you the best.

Sincerely,
Patricia A. Brownell
Executive Director

CC: Richard Forshee and Robert Bianchini

Lou Ann Talbot letter from Dallas Postal Credit Union (DPCU), December 15, 1995

Dear Florence,

I was going to wait for the pictures of the plaque dedication before I mailed this, but they are taking to long to get here! I'll send them just as soon as they arrive.

For now, I'm sending a copy of the ceremony video, along with one of our DPCU shirts and a check to reimburse your airfare.

Your presence at the plaque dedication ceremony meant more to all of us than we can ever say.

You are one of the bravest, best heroes of the Credit Union Movement. I was so delighted to meet you and share some time with you.

Again, Florence, thank you for coming. We love and respect you for all that you are.

Sincerely,
Lou Ann Talbot
Chief Operations Officer

Letter from Colleen Larney of the Southern Plains Office of Native American Programs at HUD, December 15, 1995

Dear Ms. Rogers:

Hi, my name is Colleen Larney, and I work for the Southern Plains Office of Native American Programs (HUD).

I hope you remember talking with me several months ago. When I saw your piece, "Our Heartfelt Thanks," in the July, 1995 issue of The Federal Informer.

It said everything I had not been able to say.

I called and asked if you would mind me sending it to my HUD counterparts. I've attempted to several times, and it finally made the e-mail today. I've enclosed a copy for you.

Though I haven't had the opportunity to personally meet everyone there (I take that back. I have met Lance, and he was most helpful to me), I do appreciate the kind and courteous attention I do receive when I'm in for banking transactions.

With the new year upon us, I wish each and every one of you a safe and very Happy New Year.

Thank you very much for allowing me to share your words with my counterparts.

Sincerely,

Colleen Larney

Carol Anne Burger Credit Union Times letter, January 31, 1996

Dear Florence,

Hello again my friend. I hope this letter finds you in the very best of health, knee-deep in credit union business-as-usual. It was so wonderful to see you and many of my other Oklahoma friends at CUNA's symposium in Dallas.

I must admit, as you probably already knew, this hard-nosed reporter gets mushy sometimes, too.

I'm writing to ask for whatever cooperation you can offer in my upcoming visit to Oklahoma City.

As I mentioned in our brief telephone conversation, the anniversary is approaching, and many stories will be written along the lines of "a year ago today..."

It's my hope to do that story from FECU's point of view, as best as it can be done. Unfortunately, that may mean dredging up some very sad memories.

But, I believe there is another, just as profound a story to be told. I have no preconceived notions, other than that I expect to learn something again, as I did the first time, about people and how circumstances bring out their brightest and darkest sides.

I'd like to meet with as many of those people as I interviewed before; both those who remain [at] FECU and those who have left. I'd like to meet with some members of the board and speak with some newer employees as well.

I hope I've won your trust, Florence, and I give you my assurance, that I'll do whatever I can to be as unobtrusive as possible in telling the story of FECU's survival and growth since "a year ago today..."

I look forward to seeing you again.

Sincerely,
Carol Anne Burger
Senior Writer
Credit Union Times

Florence Rogers letter to Mike Welch at the Credit Union Times, April 24, 1996

Dear Mike,

Just a note to tell you my current thoughts and to commend Carol Anne Burger.

The support of the credit union community has been outstanding, not only with our miraculous recovery, but their love and gestures for this first year following the total destruction of our office and the death of our colleagues. Your support and love also deserves kudos.

Carol Anne, as so many reporters did, became "caught up" in our story and grief. Her articles from 1995 and the follow up stories a year later were outstanding. My staff, board, and the entire credit union community have marveled at her articles and have been very touched by them. She is an excellent reporter for your publication. As you know, she was my house guest on two visits to Oklahoma. She was a delightful guest and a real friend during a "tough" time in my life. My staff and board accepted her as a part of our family during her visits. She's a great gal, Mike, and a real "keeper."

The SPECIAL EDITION she presented me on her last visit was absolutely priceless and is my favorite memento from the Oklahoma disaster. I love it, and have a good laugh every time I look at it. i have even been brave enough to show it to my special friends. (ha)

Mike, thanks for your thoughts, prayers, and caring. Hoping our paths cross again soon, I remain...

Eternally Grateful,
Florence Rogers

Florence Rogers letter to the Credit Union Foundation, CC: Bob Bianchini, President of the OK Credit Union League, July 22, 1996

Re: Nomination to Credit Union Foundation, Inc.

I am deeply honored to have been nominated for the foundation board, however, I feel that I must remove my name for this nomination for the following reasons.

My board of directors feel that this would be too time consuming since I am already out of the office [at times] telling our story to credit union related organizations.

I feel I can promote the foundation in my talks as well as if I was a board member.

When I commit to something, I do my best to give it "my all" and, at this time, I could not do that. We will never forget the wonderful work the Foundation did for us during our terrible time.

I will be serving on the Oklahoma City Memorial Foundation that has been established in relation to an international memorial to honor those who were killed, survived, and those whose lives were forever changed.

This will be a three-year project, and the foundation board is meeting monthly for several days with the design competition team that has been hired to conduct the entries for such a memorial.

Public fundraising will begin soon, and I have committed to assist with this endeavor.

Also, we will soon be launching into a building project for our permanent location of the main office.

I understand that can also be time consuming.

With the trial still looming and expected to last at least six months, I will need to be available, not only to testify, but to support the staff during what predicts to be an uncomfortable time.

Again, I am honored and would love to serve on the foundation board, but I must at this time devote my energies to the community and state where I owe my first devotion.

Respectfully,
Florence Rogers

Libby McNellis letter, May 15, 1997

Libby became a dear friend after we became acquainted through a series of calligraphy meetings over several years.

She lived in Norman, Oklahoma about 25 minutes up the road from me in Oklahoma City.

Dear Florence:

Several times over these past two years, I've seen you on

national television as well as local television programs, and I checked our old Sooner Scribes directories for your address as I wanted to write to you.

I thought for a long time [that] I knew none of the persons who were in the Alfred P. Murrah Federal Building when it was bombed over two years ago until I saw you on TV explaining what you were doing at 9:02 AM on April 19, 1995 in your office of the Federal Employees Credit Union; how the floor caved in and a number of your employees died in the explosion leaving you on an 18" ledge where you had to be rescued later.

I did not know until recently [that] you had a neck injury, but I do hope your neck is alright now and [that] all of what you went through during that time has healed somewhat. Something like that will never be forgotten.

I really listened intently when I heard your name mentioned on national TV, then again when I saw "Tapestry." The day of the bombing, a friend of mine called at 9:05 and told me to turn on my TV as something terrible has happened in Oklahoma City.

I kept glued to the TV for the rest of the day crying frequently and couldn't believe what I was seeing.

That day I'll remember always—I just could not believe anyone could do such an act, but it would take a man like Timothy McVeigh to pull something off like that. Just hope he gets what he deserves.

He left so many families losing loved ones as well as being maimed, and they will be scarred for life. I hope and pray you are OK, and I do wish you the very best in the future.

I got tired of traveling to the Will Rogers Garden Center for a monthly meeting so I no longer attend Sooner Scribes.

I retired in 1986. Bill and I travel a bit, and I'm into ceramics at the Norman Senior Citizens Center each Monday.

My recent project is six cherubs in all different positions. Last Christmas, my project was five white and gold Renaissance Santas for gifts.

I had decorated sweatshirts, and, one day, I was experimenting to see if fused material could be ironed onto card stock.

It worked, and when I go into Hancock's, I'm constantly on the lookout for material that would fuse onto cards.

Then, I calligraph a message inside. I've enjoyed doing this, and I have quite a few cards on hand for mailing such as cats, dogs, horses, frogs, flowers, Precious Moments characters, football players, teddy bears, Mickey Mouse characters, ducks, bunnies, angels, bells, golfers, penguins, etc.

I've made my Christmas cards this way for years as well as Easter and Valentine's Day cards.

The best to you always, Florence. Since you've been on my mind a lot lately, I decided I just had to write to you.

Love ,
Libby McNellis

P.S. I'll enclose one of my Christmas angel cards for you since you beat death on that dreary day.

Letter from Jeanette Gamba of Jordan Associates Advertising & Communications firm, May 26, 2006

This letter was sent to me 11 years after the bombing, but the contents are why I believe it belongs in this list of "post-bombing letters of good will.

Dear Florence,

What a delightful surprise to get your letter and the "old" newspaper. (Mercy, was I ever that young?)

I hardly knew what to say about the kind remarks in your letter. I'm simply amazed that you would have kept the article since we hadn't even met.

Isn't it incredible how our paths crossed almost a decade later?

Florence, you said I may be an inspiration to others, but you inspire me. Your courage and sensitivity are extraordinary. I observed your leadership abilities as we worked together to build the memorial and realized why you held the CEO position at the credit union.

Best wishes, my friend.
Jeannette L. Gamba
President and Chief Executive Officer

Chapter 2
Why?

Whenever a devastating event occurs whether it is a sudden death, debilitating injury, divorce, betrayal, financial woe, or even the disintegration of a friendship, one of the first and most prevalent questions we ask is: "Why?"

We wonder what the innocent party did to deserve the misfortune. The innocent party could be a "why them?" or a "why me?" Why the suffering? Why now? Why not someone else who is not so innocent? Why didn't God step in with protection?

All of these "WHYs" were swirling throughout my head as I processed the deaths of my friends, patrons, and colleagues. Undoubtedly, many more variations on the "why" questions were swirling through the minds of others who lost family members.

I think about the 19 innocent children in Heaven with the Lord right now, and I conclude that not a single one of those parents drove off from the Alfred P. Murrah Building thinking that minutes later, a maniac would drive up in a bomb laced truck in front of that same building to slaughter their son or daughter in that daycare.

My understanding is that right about that time of morning, the children would have been gathered by that big glass window seated on the carpet for story time.

One of the daycare workers was found in the rubble with a child in her lap who, no doubt, crawled up there to get a good snuggle while listening to her read. I can only imagine the infinite number of "WHYs" with a hundred question marks those parents had.

Whenever I see a school shooting on television I think of the commonality those parents have with the parents of the bombing victims.

You drop your kid off thinking they're their safe at school, and you have no idea that you'll never see their smiles again.

You won't get to drop them off at college or attend their weddings or spoil the sweet grandchildren they would have likely given you.

Why?

In Oklahoma City
Under clear blue sky
Nothing was suspicious
Nothing seemed awry.

They came to the city
Not to say "Hi"
Causing death and destruction
The question is WHY?

Do they like to hear
Little children cry
Is their conscience unplugged?
Still the question is WHY?

They hit us hard
They made us cry
They came with a vengeance.
The question...WHY?

The Ryder was parked
A coward's reply
The bomb was planted
The question...WHY?

At the Federal Building
Where many did die
How come the children?
The question is WHY?
We don't understand
But, indeed we try to
Reach a conclusion
But still we ask WHY?

They took away lives
Things money can't buy

And struck terror in hearts
Stunned, we ask WHY?

Death and destruction
At our souls pry
So very many hurting
Still the question WHY?

We hear their pain
Through a mournful sigh
Standing and waiting
With no answer WHY?

At the other side
In the sweet 'by 'n 'by
The answer will come
Because the Lord knows WHY.

--Written by Allen Moore, Cooperton, OK

The bombing was so jarring that although I have peace about God sparing my life, I can't help but roll through those why questions every now and then—but I don't stay there. I don't stay there because it takes me to a dark place.

The truth of the matter is that most of these questions will only be answered when we see the Lord, and even then, all of our tears are washed away, and we are in a place with no more sadness, so it ultimately will not matter anyway.

He will wipe away every tear from their eyes, and death shall be no more, neither shall there be mourning, nor crying, nor pain anymore, for the former things have passed away.
--Revelation 21:4 (ESV)

One book about the bombing is titled Where Was God at 9:02 A.M.? Its premise is to help people process grief and to understand why God allows (not *causes*, but *allows*) certain hardships into our lives while focusing on the inspiring stories of those who helped during the bombing.

I tend to lean more toward this angle and choose to focus on the heroes of that day and the beautiful memories of the loved ones I lost. As a Believer in Jesus Christ who attends church regularly, I believe that nothing happens by accident. All of our experiences—tragic or not—are lines in the larger blueprint of God's ultimate Will for our lives.

God knows when evil is coming. Our minds are too finite to understand His infinite knowledge and divine reasoning behind the times that He steps in to completely stop the evil and the times that He makes us go through it.

Knowing how fragile life is, I chose to take this route of thinking and to make the most of my life since God saw fit to leave me here.

I won't ever know all the reasons He spared me and left me here to grieve, but while I'm still here I try to live my life as an example of God's grace and mercy. That is ultimately how I received peace—but my healing did not happen overnight.

I wrote this book to take you through my journey, and before you understand how I process grief, tackle anxiety, and choose to live a full and productive life, you will first need to understand just how deep this situation was.

You will need to understand the heaviness of my "why questions," and you'll need to understand the numerous situations that invoked those "why questions." Only then will you understand my triumph.

Time and time again and in numerous ways, the local and national credit unions proved why we are all considered family. For example, our patrons are not merely customers as they are referred to by banks, but they are "members."

Throughout this book, you will see me mention several credit unions by name that jumped in and helped us get back on our feet at the Federal Employees Credit Union (FECU).

One of them is the Tinker Federal Credit Union who provided us a temporary location to operate in since our offices had been demolished in the bombing.

I sat in full view of everyone who walked into the temporary location of the credit union so that the members could see me as they came into an unfamiliar building.

The bombing was such a jolting tragedy that nearly everyone in Oklahoma City was shell-shocked, and I knew our members had to have been unsure if the Federal Employees Credit Union would be able to bounce back at all let alone take care of their accounts and records.

I had 33 total employees at the credit union.

Not only had 18 of them been killed, but six others were seriously injured and unable to return to work for several weeks. I wanted our members to know that I was on the job and looking after their money.

Many times as they walked in, I would stop mid-task or freeze in my tracks to pivot and go embrace members who were coming in for the first time.

Grieving Stories – The credit card

As first responders sifted through the rubble, personal items of the victims were retrieved and brought to a location very close to our temporary space at Tinker Federal Credit Union.

I would visit the location on my lunch breaks and search for things that might belong to my former employees and mementos that had belonged to my office or to people I knew.

They were very strict initially about releasing items to anyone who wasn't a family member, but as the weeks wore on, it was apparent that there was no looting and that everyone was sacred about returning the items to a rightful owner or to a family member.

There were photos, car keys, and many personal items that were kept in the desks of those employed in the now demolished building.

My purse was eventually found. It still had huge clumps of cement in it when I picked it up.

All of the traveler's checks and even some cash left over from my cruise with my sister the week before were still there as well as a bottle of cologne that I had purchased in St. Thomas which was amazingly still intact. (I talk more about this later in the section: *Grieving Stories – Sgt. Don Browning, the police dog, and my purse.*)

One day, one of my credit union members came into my office and handed me a credit card that he had found when he was sifting through the items that had been brought to the property room. He had survived the bombing also.

When he brought me that credit card, the hair on my arms stood straight up. That card had belonged to my vice president who had died from breast cancer six years earlier in 1989.

Her name was Von, and she had been the only staff member that I had lost to death before the bombing. She had retired when she became ill, and during the following years, the carpets had been changed by the General Service Administration who managed the building at least twice.

We had also replaced the furniture with brand new cubicles. That her credit card would turn up with an expiration date of April, 1988 seemed pretty strange.

I, along with the survivors who had worked under her supervision, felt like maybe Von was sending us a message from beyond somehow.

I located her children who had been living in Texas and in Oklahoma to tell them this story, but they had moved on and didn't wish to meet with me. I understood that. If their emotions were even a fraction of the emotional rollercoaster I was on, then I could understand why they didn't want to meet.

Grieving Stories – Boy Scouts Den Mother

I am a firm believer that I am the sum total of my life experiences, and I explain more specifically what I mean by this in chapter 4.

Our lives come full circle in so many ways. People who cross our paths are woven into the deeper quilt of our total life story. It's one beautiful complicated mystery of God's tapestry for our lives.

Some of my most emotional moments centered around returning purses to the family members of my 18 deceased employees. Anyone who knows a woman knows how a purse contains our "entire life" so to speak.

When the purses were brought to me, some of them would be soggy from the busted pipes or from rain. Others would have various levels of deterioration from having been buried under the building debris and damaged from the bombing materials. I could see their wallets, makeup bags, notes to themselves—things that were truly personal identifiers of the purse's owner.

One day in the midst of my returning belongings to the families of my lost geese, I came across a purse with ultrasounds sticking out of it. It had belonged to a very pregnant Robbin Huff whom I had hired as one of my loan officers. Not only was Robbin pregnant at the time of the bombing in April, but her due date was only two months later in June.

That day, I discovered that I had not only been a mother goose to Robbin but to her husband, Ronald, as well. When Ronald came to retrieve Robbin's purse, I realized that I had been his den mother when he was in cub scouts.

Ronald was a young adult eager to start a new chapter in life, but now, here he stood in front of me dealing with the sudden loss of his wife and the annihilated hope of a newborn baby that God had gifted to the two of them.

When Jesus called Satan "the thief" who "comes only to steal, and to kill, and to destroy", He had to have been referring to textbook examples like this one. *(John 10:10)* That day, I held that young man as tight as I would have held my own sons, Terry and Jerry.

Ronald's pain was palpable, and as we cried and embraced, I wanted so much—just like a mother holding a wounded child—to take away his pain. Oh, how I wished I could just "kiss it and make it better," but I couldn't. This was no boo-boo. It was a full-fledged wound that would take years to heal.

Grieving Stories – The white carnation flower

The first day we opened the credit union back up for business—just 48 hours after the bombing, a local florist delivered a personal bouquet of flowers to me from my sister, Joellyn.

Never have I felt so blessed to receive flowers, and of course, it's especially wonderful when the gift is from a family member. I needed a piece of home, some familiarity in my scary new world.

Everything felt like a whirlwind.

Not only was I still shaken from having survived the attack—and the news that it was an intentional bombing instead of a potential gas leak—but I was in an unfamiliar place with a fraction of my staff, and I had to get our operations up and running.

Tragedy or no tragedy, our members' financial security was a top priority.

We were dealing with people's livelihoods, and a number of them had been affected by the damage the bombing had done to nearby businesses, places of residence, and their own personal families re: injuries and deaths.

I felt like I could relate to them.

We now know that 18 ladies who worked for me were killed in the bombing, but at this time only two days after the bombing, they were still labeled as "missing."

The feeling of the unknown was deeply unsettling.

The card attached to the bouquet of flowers said:

"There are 18 red carnations representing your girls still missing, and the white carnation in the middle represents you. My love and sympathy to you but also my congratulations on the record recovery of the Federal Employees Credit Union.

Love, Your Sis"

Nearly every day, I convened with my directors and staff at a huge boardroom table to discuss business of the day and to convey to everyone whose bodies were most recently recovered and when and where funeral services were to be held.

I explained the significance of the flowers and placed them right in the middle of that table.

Nearly two weeks went by and, by this time, we had been notified that the 18 missing ladies were indeed 18 deceased ladies. One by one we were notified when their bodies were found. That bomb had robbed my goslings from the credit union nest.

Each day, the newspaper obituary section was filled with funeral notifications, and nearly each day, I was among the thousands of people in Oklahoma and around the world who had to decide which funeral to attend.

168 people were killed in the bombing, and when you figure the family members, friends, classmates, and colleagues of each living person, that's a lot of people descending on Oklahoma at one time to attend funerals.

There are literally no words to describe the heaviness of how something like this feels. On top of the sudden shock of losing our 18 loved ones, we were also dealing with the inability to look on their faces one last time.

Their bodies had been so disfigured and/or dismembered by the bomb, and, in some cases decayed by the time they were recovered, that all of the funerals were closed casket services. We were deprived of that closure.

That was true for most of the additional 150 people who were killed as well.

This tragedy was so devastating that one mother who lost her baby in the explosion said that, in one aspect, she felt fortunate that at least she had some closure by being able to view her child's body because she knew that the majority of other parents were not afforded that opportunity.

That's how bad it was.

One major aspect of the grief we experienced at the Federal Employees Credit Union is that we knew a good number of the 168 people who died.

Aside from the 19 children who had perished in the daycare, the majority of those who were killed were federal employees who worked for a government agency on one of the nine floors of the building.

Many of whom had accounts with us, and were thereby members of our credit union.

We considered them all family. On any given day, hundreds of those who worked in the building would frequent our office for a transaction.

We would run into them on the 4th floor in the snack bar or on the elevator or on the way into work. It was our own little community. You could actually say that I knew over 100 of the 168 lost by name.

On the morning of the bombing, three members of our credit union who were not government employees were in our office, and they too perished that morning along with our 18 lost employees: Alvin Justes, Woodrow "Woody" Brady, and Sheila Driver whom we believe were making deposits into and retrieving funds from their accounts.

(By the way, in 2019, 24 years after the bombing, I discovered that the fireman in the famous bombing photo cradling a deceased 1 year-old baby was actually with Sheila in her final hours. His name is Chris Fields, and he too has a book in this *Beauty for Ashes* series titled *Out of Chaos* where he details his emotional encounter with Sheila.)

As I said...this was a very heavy emotional time. Those flowers from my sister (18 red carnations representing the ladies and the white carnation representing me) were a welcome vision of light in the midst of a continuous stream of dark news.

Late one quiet night, around that "two week post-bombing mark," I was working late in our temporary office, and everyone had gone home. By this time, I had received confirmation of the last of the 18 recovered bodies. I heard the cleaning lady coming down the hallway pulling her trash can and running her vacuum.

Then, I suddenly remembered that the bouquet my sister gifted me had been moved to a credenza in the board room because they had started to wilt. I dashed over to the board room to retrieve it because I had wanted to save the lovely vase they were in, and I didn't want the cleaning lady to mistake the vase as trash.

Since it was getting late, I just bundled up the entire vase with the wilting flowers and carried them to my car. When I got home, I sat them on my dining room table along with many others that I had received and forgot about them.

A couple of more weeks went by, and one day I noticed that all of the 18 carnations were dry and brittle, but the white carnation was still as fresh as the day they were sent.

I couldn't believe it. I took pictures of it. It was like even nature knew that my 18 precious employees, friends, and goslings had been taken from me, but I was left here to grieve them and help care for their families.

Even after I took those photos, the white carnation lived on until I finally threw all of them away.

Grieving Stories – The Puppy

I hired Tresia Mathes Worton in October of 1994, just six months before the bombing in April, so she was one of the newer employees who perished in the tragedy. Tresia was 28 and single. Her hometown was Midland, TX where her family was still living.

The bombing occurred on Wednesday, April 19, 1995, and on Monday, April 17, Tresia had given us her two-week notice to leave. She was needed back in Midland to help with care for her ailing grandmother.

We didn't have a lot of information on her family including contact information, so we ended up calling the apartment manager where she lived to check on her newly acquired puppy.

She planned to take that sweet little dog with her back to Midland when she left Oklahoma City, and now it had lost its owner. I was never able to meet any of her family members. This is a very sad memory for me.

Grieving Stories – The Cat

27 year-old Jill Randolph was one of my accountants at the credit union. Jill perished in the bombing, but remember at the time, we weren't sure who would and wouldn't be found alive.

When I made it home the day of the bombing, my son, Terry, and I started calling the apartments and homes of those who were yet unaccounted for to make sure there was no pets inside that were left unattended.

Jill was single with no roommate, and her parents lived in Tulsa, so there was no one who would have been able to tell anyone about a pet.

Therefore, I'm glad Terry and I made these calls because, sure enough, Jill had a large cat in her apartment.

I love animals, and the thought of this cat never seeing its owner again is still so sad to me.

Jill had the sweetest countenance, and her personality matched. I'm sure that big ole cat had a soft heart that needed mending after losing her.

Grieving Stories – Jason Smith's Mama

The bomb ripped through all nine floors of the Alfred P. Murrah building leaving each organization's workspace uninhabitable including our credit union office. Tinker Federal Credit Union stepped up and quickly allotted us that temporary workspace.

Not long after that, Tinker moved into a brand new building in Bethany, and we were able to transition into the site they had vacated. This was such a blessing. The location suited all of our present needs to begin the task of rebuilding the credit union.

We had been thankful for the original makeshift location that Tinker allotted for us, but we sure were happy to finally move into our new fully functioning office space.

Amidst all the loss and tragedy, a new space allowed us to start to feel more like a credit union again. We were saddled with a "to do list" that felt like it had the length of the equator and the depth of the Pacific Ocean.

Remember that along with the 18 deceased credit union employees, many of the remaining 150 who were killed were also members of the credit union because they were federal employees.

Therefore, you can understand that we were incredibly busy:

- handling insurance claims
- hiring new employees to fill our staff needs
- dealing with those on our staff who survived and had workers comp claims
- fielding constant calls from members concerning their accounts
- contacting families of our lost employees whenever someone brought one of their personal items discovered among the rubble.

People all over the United States saw the horrific videos and images of the bombing on daily and nightly national news coverage, and inundated us with donations.

Fellow credit union organizations and even people around the world sent hordes of gifts to us. I even saw packages from Canada, and Australia.

We were grateful that so many people cared, but the process of managing the gifts along with these emotional outpourings, on top of the workload, was all so overwhelming.

During this incredibly busy time, I hired a new administrative assistant. Her name was Lori Wilson, and she was so good at deterring the constant interruptions that took up so much of my time.

42 days into our stint at the new location, a young man who appeared to be in his upper teen years started coming in every few days wanting to talk to me.

I repeatedly instructed Lori that I couldn't possibly take time to talk to this person and that she should send him away.

The young man didn't give up.

One day after several of his visits, I caught a glimpse of him through my office window. He was in the lobby waiting patiently for his chance to see if I was finally going to talk to him, so I weakened and told Lori to go ahead and let him in.

What was so urgent that he was insisting on seeing me?

He introduced himself as Jason Smith and explained to me that his mother, Linda McKinney, was killed in the bombing. Jason felt that I might have been the last person to have spoken with her.

Linda worked for the Secret Service on the top floor of the 9-floor Murrah Building. Jason knew that she also served on our credit union's "Credit Committee."

Sure enough, I had sat with Linda at our monthly credit union chapter social event on April 18, 1995, the exact evening before the terrible morning of the bombing, and she and I had talked through the entire meal and program.

I was immediately filled with compassion for Jason. This young man had been devastated over Linda's death.

I could tell that he was so lost and just needed someone to talk to about his mother. In instances of sudden loss due to tragedy, it is not unusual for family members to form a bond with whoever was the last person to speak to their deceased loved one.

It's their way of trying to get a grasp on the final moments of that loved one's life since they were deprived of a proper closure.

Linda and I had known each other for several years. As a member of our credit committee, Linda was one of five people who were tasked with approving larger loans.

The five credit committee members would stop by often to ask if their approval was needed so as not to hold up the process. Therefore, I saw Linda quite frequently in the credit union office.

The credit committee was a non-compensated volunteer position elected by credit union members which meant that Linda did it as an act of service. She was a great asset to our business.

I proceeded to tell Jason how much I thought of his wonderful mother.

I told him that Linda was the sweetest person and that we really appreciated the work she did for the credit committee.

She did everything we asked and contributed to the culture of great customer service that we prided ourselves on at the credit union. I had thought so much of her.

Then, just as I had hugged Ronald Huff, I wrapped up a heart-broken Jason in the tightest "mama hug" I could muster.

Jason eventually moved from Oklahoma City to another state to be closer to his father.

He has a beautiful wife and adorable daughter and has a great career in telecommunications. We remain connected, and I value our special friendship.

Grieving Stories – Sgt. Browning, the police dog, and my 1st cry

For months after the bombing, several of my friends, family, and credit union associates asked me if I was in counseling or if I'd had time to have a really good cry.

My reply to them usually sounded something like: "No, I really don't feel that I need counseling. I have family and close friends that I can lean on, and besides, I don't have time right now to take the time to cry. Maybe this fall when things settle down a bit."

After the bombing, I was blessed with incredible strength that I didn't know I had. My sons, Terry and Jerry, even started calling me the "Stalwart Woman." It has been said that a person doesn't know how strong they are until they have no other alternative.

Indeed, as I worked to rebuild the credit union and battle grief, I often felt as if the weight of the entire Murrah Building rubble rested on my shoulders. I perceived that my options were either to function and move forward or to fold and break, and I had no interest in folding and breaking.

However, on August 3rd, some months later, I was informed by my Vice President, Raymond Stroud, that an Oklahoma City police officer was waiting on the phone anxious to speak with me. I took the call, and it was a conversation I will never forget. It was almost 4:30pm in the afternoon, and my day was not nearly over considering the long hours that I had put into the office those weeks and months.

A man whose voice was struggling through sobs said: "Florence Rogers, it is so good to hear your voice. I have wanted to talk to you for so long now, but we were advised by our supervisor not to bother the survivors until some time has passed."

He then told me he was Sergeant Don Browning with the Oklahoma City Police Department and that he and his search dog, Gunny, had found my purse not long after they had been allowed on the scene of the bombing to assist with the rescue/recovery efforts. Gunny had located my purse in the rubble.

It contained a big bottle of cologne that I had purchased from one of the duty free shops on the cruise that my sister and I had just returned from.

Sergeant Browning felt that Gunny's discovery of my purse taught him the types of smells that he was supposed to sniff out.

A woman's purse is so very personal, and its contents can reveal a lot about its owner.

My purse also contained a big pile of the cruise photos that I had developed and intended to mail to my sister.
(Remember, there were no iPhones or text messages then!)

Sergeant Browning explained that Gunny had found my purse nearby two bodies: a woman, and one of the deceased 19 children. It was a stark reminder to him that those items were not just items.

Real people and real lives were attached to them. Sergeant Browning looked through the purse, saw the cruise photos, and ended up writing my name, birth date, and SS number on his brand new pair of light tan leather gloves.

My purse was a conduit that created a personal connection to him.

A few days after the bombing, as Sergeant Browning worked search and rescue, he told his crew that they "need to concentrate on finding the body of Florence Rogers."

They told him: "She had made it out of the building and was included in a newspaper article the first weekend after the bombing along with two other women, a nurse, and a mother."

Between sobs, Sergeant Browning told me how for months, he had wanted to personally let me know how glad and relieved he was to learn that I had made it out alive.

All the time Sergeant Browning was telling me his story, I could feel the water welling in my eyes. When we finally hung up, I knew that I had to leave the office and shed those inevitable tears.

I grabbed my new purse and told Raymond that I had to leave. I sobbed all the way home which was a 16 mile drive and continued long into the evening. I could not stop weeping.

About 9pm that night, my brother, Don, called me, and he could tell when I answered the phone that I was not in good shape. I told him it was one of the worst days I'd had so far.

He volunteered to come to my home to comfort me, but I told him I thought I was going to be okay, and we kept talking long enough for me to settle down from all the tears.

I thanked Don a bunch for being so sweet and helping his little sister get through that rough day and evening.

A few years after the bombing, a news agency from London was in town doing some stories about the Oklahoma City Bombing.

They had heard about Sergeant Browning's dog finding my purse and how great his dog, Gunny, had been at the task of locating the victims.

The agency arranged a surprise for me, and when I arrived downtown for the interview, I finally got to meet Sergeant Browning and Gunny in person.

Sergeant Browning showed me the gloves on which he'd written my personal information and stated that he was going to give them to the Oklahoma City National Memorial & Museum archives. Many thanks to Sergeant Browning for giving me that most healing cry.

Grieving Stories – The Penny

Grief is an interesting experience. When most people hear the term, the focus is on emotions, but it can actually have any number of mental and physical effects as well.

Not only that, but a popular book was published about the so-called five stages of grief, and it seemed to somewhat simplify grief—mostly around emotionally based aspects. However, the truth of the matter is that grief is much more complicated, and you might experience waves of it at various times of your life long after you've experienced the so-called five stages that the book focuses on.

Don't misunderstand me. I'm not bashing the book, and there are several things the authors get right, but, again, the book seems to simplify grief when in fact grief is a very complex thing that all of us will endure at some point or another, and we will all process it in our own unique ways.

This is especially true when you've survived an event as traumatic as the Oklahoma City Bombing. You might be just fine one moment, and then a wave of grief may overcome you when you have a thought or a reminder of that horrible day.

It doesn't mean that I haven't processed my grief or that I'm not yet through all the "stages" of grief. It's just something I have to deal with, and the key is to not be consumed with a spirit of grief that permanently paralyzes me emotionally, mentally, physically, and spiritually.

Ecclesiastes 3:4 says there is "a time to mourn" and there may be many times throughout life. It doesn't mean that I haven't processed my grief or "graduated from the stages." It means that I am human. When it happens, God always seems to send me an "out" so that I don't wallow in it.

In early 2004, that "out" was a penny.

One day, around that year's anniversary of the bombing, I was preparing one of my many speeches for some organization or anniversary event. I don't exactly remember which one.

As I would write some of my speech, I found that the horrifying memories of that dreadful day and the dreadful death notifications would come flooding back, and I would have to take occasional breaks from my writing.

I would get up from my desk and take both of my little dogs down to the creek area near my home. We would walk around and breathe the fresh air while I tried to forget that terrible day in my life.

The grass was still brown and dead since spring was a few weeks ahead.

One day, on one of my writing breaks, the dogs and I were walking along the creek bank, and a beautiful sight stopped me in my tracks.

In the middle of the brown and dead grass, I saw the sun shining on something bright and colorful. When I went to see what it was, I could hardly believe what I'd found.

It was a tiny, gorgeous, satin purse in perfect condition. I have no idea how it got there or how long it had been there. When I opened it up, I was shocked to find that the only thing inside of it was a bright shiny 1995 penny—the same year as the bombing nine years prior.

I considered it a sign from above: a kiss from heaven saying: "I'm still with you Florence. In all of the pain and tragedy, I am still going to bring you beauty from those ashes." (Isaiah 61:3)

After that, I was inspired to create a special memento containing a 1995 penny so that we will never forget April 19, 1995. The memento could be used as a bookmark or just as a reminder of a day that forever changed so many lives in Oklahoma and around the world.

After several of my speeches, I handed out those little mementos until I ran out of the 1995 pennies.

Grieving Stories – Girlfriend the Chihuahua

I was single at the time of the bombing. I had owned a Chihuahua dog named "Girlfriend" since she was a puppy, but my ex-husband took her with him after he left.

Once he remarried, he discovered that his new wife didn't much like dogs. Since he worked on the first floor of the Murrah building, and I worked on the third floor, he took the opportunity one workday to come up two floors to tell me he was giving Girlfriend back to me.

I was so happy hearing his words that I burst into tears knowing that I would soon have that sweet girl sitting on my lap again.

I didn't know it at the time, but Girlfriend would prove to be a wonderful and much needed companion to me. Not long after she came back to live with me, the bombing killed so many of my employees and patrons of the credit union. She was such a blessing.

Each day, when I would leave my house for another day of the daunting task of rebuilding the credit union, I would leave Girlfriend on my bed. She would still be on the bed on my pillow when I got home as if to assure me: "I'm going to be right here for you when you get back."

My usual routine after arriving back home was to head into the living room, plop down on the couch, and try to watch something on TV.

Girlfriend would crawl up into my lap, and I would hold her. The bombing happened in April, but I didn't have a full "cry" for my lost friends and employees until August of that year.

It was like I didn't want to allow myself to feel everything for fear that I would shut down and be unable to function.

Just 48 hours after the bombing, the credit union was back up and running in temporary location, so I immediately got to work. There was no time to get lost in my emotions...right?

I am no psychologist, but when that heavy of an emotional weight is on you, it doesn't matter how hard you work to mask it, it will find a way to manifest itself.

That is what happened with me and my sweet little dog. I would bury my head on her back, weep, and say through tears: "I'm sorry that I haven't been here all day, Girlfriend."

At the time I didn't admit it—and I'm not sure I fully realized it—but those tears really had nothing to do with me leaving *my dog* alone all day.

Those tears were because 18 of "my girls" had left *me* alone. They were amazing employees, close friends, and just overall good people.

They were my goslings, and they left the nest without warning. A few of them had actually become some of my closest friends on earth. Our relationships had extended past surface work friendships to mother-daughter type friendships and/or big sister/little sister friendships.

Again, it took until August of 1995—four months after the actual bombing—for me to succumb to all of my emotions and really have a good cry for all who had died, but at this time, I had not consciously connected my tears to the deceased. I just told myself that I was crying for having left Girlfriend alone all day.

Dogs really are some of the best companions to humans. Girlfriend was my best friend during this time period. She was always glad to see me.

Always a joyful source of support and carefree love. Always there. The emptiness of my home seemed more noticeable after the bombing, and she brought life to my empty home as the silence seemed more deafening.

We would take walks around the neighborhood anytime I could. She lived to be 17 years old and I had enjoyed her comfort and love for nine more years after the bombing losing her in December, 2004.

Grieving Stories – A Final Funeral Four Years Later

For about a month straight, there was a funeral every day for the 168 innocent people killed in the bombing—many times, there were multiple funerals in a day. I attended many of them, and it was a grueling process. Naturally, I thought that after the last of our deceased bombing victims had been buried, I was done attending funerals for a while, but, four years later, I found myself attending one final bombing-related funeral.

On the morning of Saturday, December 11, 1999, about 100 mourners paid respects as a casket holding the unidentified remains of the victims of the Alfred P. Murrah Federal Building was buried.

The casket contained mostly small fragments of tissue, bone and hair that had been stored in the medical examiner's office since the explosion and had not been matched with the specific bodies to which they had once belonged. A limb that had been buried in the wrong grave and later exhumed was also included.

I had been asked to serve on the "tissue committee" to decide what should be done with these fragments, and we decided to preserve the dignity of those who had perished by holding an actual funeral service for the additional remains.

As gruesome as this may sound, the 1999 service actually brought a sense of closure to the medical examiner's office and to those who might have been in a state of shock during the sudden whirlwind of funerals of their loved ones four years prior. It was like another chance to have a memorial service for them with a more settled mind. Pieces of them were "still here," and they needed to be laid to rest.

The casket was buried on the Oklahoma State Capitol grounds among a grove of 168 linden trees representing those people who had died.

Grieving Stories –Freedom From Survivor's Guilt

I traveled the globe after the Oklahoma City Bombing telling my story of survival and how in my 25th year, I led the rebirth of Federal Employees Credit Union in what proved to be the toughest challenge of my career.

Indeed, nowhere in the hiring process did anyone say: "Florence, you will have to lead the reopening of this financial institution for our 16,000 members only 48 hours after the devastating attack. Can you do that?" Surely, I would have turned down the job opportunity and headed for another credit union, but God had different plans. I believe this is part of why we can't see the future. God knows if we could, we'd run from our destinies.

I was often asked two questions during/after those presentations:

1.) Did you suffer from survivor's guilt?
2.) How does one grieve over 18 lost employees all at once?

First, I'll address the survivor's guilt. Survivor's guilt is when a person feels they have done something wrong because they survived an incident—usually a tragedy--when others did not. It is often listed as one of the symptoms of post-traumatic stress disorder (PTSD).

Many, many times in the weeks and months following the bombing, I was asked if I felt any survivor's guilt after coming so close to my own death and losing so many of the staff of the credit union. A few of the remaining staff members did suffer from survivor's guilt. They had either been away from the office at the time of the explosion or had managed to survive their injuries.

I never experienced anything that felt like survivor's guilt because I told myself that God had saved me for a purpose, and I have consistently maintained that mindset. On top of which, I was mentally consumed with leading the process of rebuilding the credit union. It was also very important to me to honor my lost employees by doing that as best as I knew how. I truly felt that if those ladies could speak to us from beyond that is exactly what they would tell us to do. It was almost like I could hear Vicky Texter, my former Visa Program Manager, using her signature phrase: "Do everything with excellence." I sure missed her during the rebuilding process. She was a great hire.

However, even with the emotional distraction of burying myself in my work, I still believe that it is possible that I could have experienced survivor's guilt had it not been for one late night phone call I received from Sheila Stroud, the mother of Sonja Sanders.

27 year-old Sonja was my Chief Teller of Operations when she was killed. She was the mother of two little girls, one of whom was a toddler. That night on the phone, Sheila told

me how very glad she was that I had survived. I will never forget the heartfelt way she spoke to me through her sobs. I too became emotional. I told Sheila that her call meant quite a lot to me because I knew she had to feel overwhelmed not only with the loss of her daughter but with facing the possibility of raising two precious granddaughters who had lost their mother.

Sheila along with her other daughter and Sonja's sister, Kristi, and Kristi's husband did such a great job raising Sonja's two girls who had been given "city names" Brooklyn and Savanna. I address them as the "city girls" whenever I see them around town. As I write this, one of them is now working at our credit union, and the other one is married with a one year-old.

Grieving Stories – 18 Memories

Now to answer the second question: "How does one grieve over 18 lost employees all at once?" You really cannot grieve that many people at once. It is too much to process. However, one by one as the weeks passed, each one of those employees was brought to mind by a memory or circumstance, and I shed special specific tears for that particular one. Here is a recap of the special grieving moments I had for each of those ladies.

VALERIE KOELSCH

I hired Valerie March 21, 1983, when she was 22 years old and just graduating from OSU with a degree in Marketing. I had been approved by the board of directors to hire an Administrative Assistant/Marketing Director. My personal workload had become quite heavy due to my handling of most of the marketing of the credit union. On top of which, the credit union had grown substantially.

I knew about Valerie long before I had ever seen her in person, as her dad Harry Koelsch was a volunteer board member at another credit union in the downtown area, and I often saw him at various credit union meetings and workshops. Harry had mentioned to me a few times that I should consider hiring his daughter when she graduated from college. I kept that in mind and contacted her when the approval came from my board members to fill the position.

Valerie "had me at hello" to quote a favorite movie of mine. She and I had a special bond through the years, and she was often accused by some of the other staff members that she "brown nosed" the boss.

Valerie was a devout Catholic, and each year during the lent season, I knew that every Friday, she would be standing over my desk at lunchtime telling me to stop what I was doing because we were going to go eat fish. I would grumble some, but all the while grabbing my purse.

Valerie was quite a sports fan and she would grab the sports page from my newspaper the minute I would arrive at the office, or when she came in.

She knew all the teams and kept up with all of them and could quote their standings in a heartbeat. Her mom told me that Val and her brothers played catch in their backyard every day that she could talk them into it.

We worked on the 3rd floor of the building. When the weather permitted, the babies and pre-school children on the 2nd floor daycare center would go outside to play in the little fenced-in area just outside my window where I had a great view.

Valerie would tell me to stop what I was doing and watch the babies roll and tumble and play--some of them just beginning to walk. They were always beautifully dressed and so cute.

A little brother and sister with bright red hair that glistened when the sun was out were quite easy to spot from all the others. Nineteen of those sweet little ones died. The red heads survived.

Valerie and I were both single for a time.

In addition to being an excellent employee, she became a dear friend as well. We often attended social events together, and she would end up staying overnight in my home.

My two sons, Terry and Jerry, are the joy of my life, but I never had a girl, so Valerie was like the daughter I'd never had.

Terry and Jerry were also fond of her like a little sister, but Valerie had a little crush on Jerry...She didn't want to be his sister; she wanted to be his girlfriend!

Valerie never missed sending me birthday cards, Christmas cards, Boss' Day cards and Valentine's Day cards. My home contains many gifts and mementos she gave me through the years including a Christmas ornament that I still use and treasure.

Valerie was in her eleventh year of employment when she was killed. She was loved by all of the staff, not just me. She left behind many special memories to all who knew her. I can't even watch an OSU football or basketball game without thinking of that sports-loving Valerie.

I said earlier that I didn't mourn all 18 of my deceased employees at once and that each one had their special day where I processed my grief for them, but I feel sure that I grieved for "my gal Val" for more than one day.

KIMBERLY BURGESS

Kim was hired in January, 1994 as my administrative assistant. Valerie Koelsch had served in that capacity, but she also handled marketing and had taken on the regulatory compliance issues and regulations and was quite busy.

Therefore, I needed to hire someone whose full focus was to be my assistant, and along came Kim Burgess looking for a job in Oklahoma City.

Kim was 29 years old and had just married a young man, Damon, in November of 1993 in Denver, where she and her family were living.

Damon's Air Force career took them to South Carolina, and finally to Oklahoma City's Tinker Air Force Base. I hadn't had time to really get to know Kim very well since her tenure with the credit union only lasted a year and three months before she was taken from us, but I still have fond memories of her.

Kim was always happy and very outgoing. Every time I would prepare to leave the office for a trip, she would ask me if she could clean my desk off while I was gone. My reply to her was always "not to touch a thing."

My desk might have appeared a bit messy, but I knew where everything was! I met Kim's wonderful parents at a memorial service for her that was held at the Tinker Air Force Base chapel soon after her body had been found.

Damon was devastated, and for months, he carried their wedding album tucked under his arm everywhere he went. The day I grieved for Kim was a day I spotted a young man in an Air Force uniform with a file folder tucked under an arm. Kim's parents seldom miss an anniversary event at the Oklahoma City National Memorial & Museum, and we have stayed in touch through the years and usually meet for dinner when they are in Oklahoma. I also think of Kim often when I look at my untidy desk.

KATHY FINLEY

Kathy Finley was age 44 at the time of her death and had one daughter, Melissa. Kathy was hired as a teller on June 3, 1974, and she was in her 21st year at the credit union when she was killed. Kathy rose through the ranks from a teller, to bookkeeper to Vice President of operations. In 1988, Kathy married Riley, a pilot for the U.S. Marshalls Service. They were so happy and were living the good life in a lovely home in Yukon.

Kathy was always seen dressed to the nines with those beautiful high heel shoes every day. My best memory of Kathy was when she thought she might be late to work due to traffic on the crosstown expressway.

She would take an alternate route and would feel good as long as her car was moving. The day I found myself grieving for Kathy was a day I encountered a traffic jam and had to take a detour.

Being the wife of a United States Marshal, Kathy's body was covered with a United States flag when she was found and brought out of the Murrah Building rubble.

JAMIE GENZER

Jamie was a 32 year-old single mom to Kyle and Krista when she was killed. She had only worked for 2 ½ years at our credit union. We had hired her as a loan officer, but she was already in training to become a manager. Her family was a "credit union family," so she was a natural for the position. Jamie's mother, Nancy Fialkowski, was a CEO at another credit union, and Jamie's brother was working at another credit union as the IT manager. Jamie was a very physically attractive woman with a beautiful personality to match. She loved music, sang bass for the Sweet Adelines, and was part of a quartet. Before Jamie died, the Sweet Adelines had published a cookbook with her sketched picture on the cover, and Jamie gave me a copy with a sweet note from her just inside that cover. The day I grieved for Jamie was the day I spotted that cookbook on display in my kitchen when I was preparing to bake a cake.

COLEEN HOUSLEY

Coleen, age 53, was hired as a loan officer on the 9th day of August, 1993, so her tenure with the credit union was short lived when she died on April 19, 1995.

Coleen sought employment with us at the credit union equipped with a great resume and great references.

One such reference was her husband, Gary, who had been her boss for some time at another Oklahoma City credit union.

When their marriage was on the horizon, she knew she should look for another place to work, so she came to us at FECU and was hired immediately. Coleen's and Gary's blended marriage gave them five children, and nine grandchildren with numbers ten and eleven on the way.

Coleen loved her job and was a great asset in the loan department having had an extended background in lending regulations. The day I found myself grieving for Coleen was on a day that I was driving past the credit union building where Gary still worked as its CEO, and I knew that he was inside grieving his wife also.

ROBBIN HUFF

Robbin, age 37, holds special memories to so many of us whom she left behind. She was expecting her first baby in June 1995—just two months after the bombing.

She was hired by our credit union on January 16, 1989 giving her six years and three months in tenure, and she was serving as a loan officer for us at the time of her death.

Robbin was married to Ron who had been one of my Cub Scouts when I was a den mother, and he was a high school Boy Scout student along with my sons, Jerry and Terry.

When Ron and Robbin married, Robbin became the step-mother to his two sons Corey and Matthew. They were all so excited to learn that they were going to have a baby daughter and sister to add to the family.

The day I grieved for Robbin came on a very sad day when I had called Ron to come pick up her purse that had been retrieved from the rubble. (I gave the full version of this story earlier in the chapter.) Ron fell to his knees sobbing when he first saw the horrible looking damaged purse.

The purse was partially torn open due to being wet for so long. Not only had the building pipes burst, but it had rained for several days. Sticking out of the purse was the film from the ultrasound that Robbin had brought to the office on April 19th to share with her coworkers. Ron and Robbin were going to name their daughter Amber Denise.

CHRISTI JENKINS

Christi, age 32 and mother of 4, was hired as a teller August 5th, 1985. She was in her 10th year of employment when she perished.

Christi was very involved, along with her husband in evangelistic outreach of their church. Her children were always her top priority.

The week before the bombing, when I was preparing to go on that cruise with my sister, Christi told me she would love to have a bottle of cologne since I would be in duty free shops at some point on my trip. She wrote it down and gave me the note so I wouldn't forget.

It was Dolce & Gabbana. I carefully packed the huge bottle in my luggage and safely brought it to Christi. She was so excited and tried her best to pay me for it, but I wouldn't allow her.

The day I grieved for Christi was a day when I was strolling through Dillard's to purchase some makeup and came across the Dolce & Gabbana display. To this day, I still think of Christi when I see the name Dolce & Gabbana.

KATHY LEINEN

Kathy, age 47, was a collection officer at the credit union. Her hire date was March 21, 1983 making her tenure twelve years.

She had a son and a daughter, William and Dawn. Kathy was a young grandmother to Dawn's son, Frankie, whom she adored.

Frankie and Dawn lived with Kathy for five years which meant she had more opportunities to really spoil Frankie like only a grandmother can. Kathy loved her job, and she especially enjoyed it whenever it intersected with law enforcement since she had many friends in law enforcement agencies.

The last office Christmas party before the bombing was held in my home. An unexpected heavy frost occurred during the party, and Kathy suffered a nasty fall on a railroad timber that divided my yard from the next door neighbors. She broke her collarbone, and had to be taken to the emergency room by some of the other staff members. As they drove

Kathy to the nearest emergency room, Victoria Texter threw one of my Afghans around her to protect her from the cold air that had moved in.

Not long after Kathy was killed, I was sitting in my living room and reached for something to cover my legs and feet.

When I realized that it was the same afghan that had covered Kathy that night, I buried my face in it and grieved for Kathy. It still held the smell of that last office Christmas party when we were all in flight to the same destination as one dedicated team.

CLAUDETTE MEEK

Claudette, age 43, was in her 14th year at the credit union and was the VP of Financial Services.

She was the mother of Michelle and Robert and wife of Mike. She was always referred to by the entire staff as the "cheerleader," a description so prevalent in her staff meetings where she brought food as encouragement to all attendees. Claudette treasured her job and was always happy.

Her very loud laughs were infectious and could usually be heard all over our various offices. The first day that I remember grieving for Claudette was when I was reaching for a bowl in my kitchen.

As I was pulling it down, I felt something behind the bowl and didn't know what it could possibly be.

I got a small stool out of the garage in order to see what it was. It was a Christmas Santa sleigh that Claudette had made for the entire staff that last Christmas when we were all together. The sleigh was made from candies and a lot of chocolate, and I had apparently tucked it in the house so it would not melt in my attic with the other Christmas decorations. Claudette had poured her heart into those sleighs and had stayed up way past midnight to complete them for the staff. The thought of her huge heart certainly brought on the tears as I held on to that little treasure. I think of Claudette every time I hear someone that exhibits her big laugh.

FRANKIE MERRELL

Frankie, age 23, hired as a teller, had been with us at the credit union for three and ½ years. She was a wife to Charles and took special pride in being a mother to her daughter, Morgan. Frankie was a great asset on the teller line because she loved all of the members who would wait for her to transact their business. Frankie's teller drawer containing her "beginning cash" was the first of the credit union items found in the early stages of the recovery efforts. As I walked through a grocery store one day, I noticed a pretty little mama with a baby on her hip that reminded me of sweet Frankie, and that was the day I grieved for her.

JILL RANDOLPH

Jill, age 27, had been the Certified Public Accountant for us at the credit union.

She had graduated cum laude and arrived to us with an impressive degree in accounting. Jill had only been employed for 1 year and 4 months when she was killed.

Since Jill was supervised by the VP of the Accounting Division, always busy with her job, and was a "quiet type," I didn't know her very well. Jill was one of the eight employees who were meeting in my office the morning of the bombing where we were preparing for the upcoming annual audit by our regulatory agency, the Oklahoma State Banking Department. (I detail the bombing morning story in chapter 1.) The reports that the Oklahoma State Banking Department had requested for their audit was paramount in the accounting division and Jill would play an important role in the audit.

The day I grieved for Jill was during a stop at a Dollar General Store on my way home from work. There was a huge cat lying outside of the store in the sunshine. Jill had been known by all of the credit union staff as the owner of Rascal, her humongous fifteen pound cat.

CLAUDINE RITTER

Claudine, age 48, was a very effective collection officer for our credit union. She had worked for us eight years and two months. She was a single mom to Valerie and Brian.

Claudine was a decorated soldier having served at the Pentagon in the Gulf War. She had remained in the Army National Guard after her enlistment ended and was in her thirtieth year of Army service at the time of her death.

Claudine and Brian lived together in a rural area of Moore. Brian had just barely turned 18 when she was killed. The agent in charge of the FBI, at that time, assisted me with the proper agencies to successfully award benefits to this young man since he normally would not have been entitled to benefits at his age. (One of the letters in chapter 1 references this.)

Brian was so lost after his mom's death. He would call me quite often, usually late at night as he mourned his mom and was left with so many decisions that he needed advice for. I mourned for Claudine on more than one specific day or instance mainly due to the multiple interactions with Brian. I did my best to guide Brian through a lot of issues he faced on an almost daily basis, so I was regularly reminded of Claudine.

Brian later began his career in the law enforcement field that he and his mom were so supportive of.

He took advantage of the education benefits that were available to the families and survivors of the bombing.

He first became a police officer in Moore, Oklahoma, where he and his mom had lived and has always stayed in law enforcement jobs.

He has recently graduated from the University of Texas with a Bachelor of Arts Degree in Criminology. We still talk often and stay in touch. He has made me proud.

KARAN SHEPHERD

Karan, age 28, had been a single mom living with her mother, Shirley, and daughter, Brittany, for several years before she married Jay.

Karen and Jay then gave Brittany a sister, Gabby. Karan was hired as a loan officer at age 21, on October 17, 1988, making her the youngest loan officer in the history of our credit union.

She was in her seventh year of employment.

Karan took her job seriously and could always be counted on to excel in her position.

After her death, a high number of credit union members named Karan as their favorite loan officer. I lost count of how many members relayed how much they missed her.

The day I mourned for Karan was a day that I was scrolling through my television trying to find something to watch, when I ran across a very old rerun of a Roy Rogers and Gabby Hayes movie. I immediately thought of Karan who had named her daughter Gabby.

When her mother was alive, Gabby, along with several other little ones that belonged to the staff would run into my office and jump on my lap when their moms brought them to the credit union office.

I have happily watched many of them become adults and have little ones of their own.

VIRGINIA THOMPSON

Virginia, age 58, was hired by our credit union on January 23, 1995, 18 days after her birthday on January 5th.

She had previously been the CEO of the Rock Island Credit Union in El Reno, OK where she lived.

Virginia was the mother of two sons, Phillip and Kenneth, and a daughter, Shelley. She was also a grandmother.

Virginia had decided that she wanted a change in her life, so she came to me asking if I would hire her no matter what the position was. I had known Virginia for many years throughout our many encounters at various credit union meetings and workshops.

I told her I only had a receptionist position that she might fill at the time. She said: "Great. I want to work for you."

Virginia was one of the happiest employees that I had ever encountered in my career. She would answer our phone with a smile that showed everyone who called how happy she was.

She often told me how good she felt when she left El Reno and drove to Oklahoma City every morning watching the sun rise in the east.

The day I grieved for Virginia was during a morning drive to an early meeting in Tulsa. I realized that I was watching the sun rise just like Virginia had talked about so often.

I still think of her comment whenever I am blessed enough to witness a beautiful sunrise.

VICTORIA TEXTER

Victoria (most of us called her Vicki) was age 37. She was the wife of James and mother of James III. Vicki was hired as a teller at the credit union in September 1981.

She was in her 14th year with us, and she had risen from a teller position to the VISA program manager.

Our credit union members loved Victoria, particularly the ones who needed her advice concerning their financial issues with their credit cards.

I could always count on Victoria to do her job well, and she needed very little supervision. The day I grieved for Victoria was the day I needed to use my VISA credit card at a department store to charge a purchase. I still think of Victoria at times when I reach for my VISA card.

TRESIA MATHES-WORTON

Tresia, age 28, was hired by our credit union on October 3, 1994, which means she had only been with us as a teller for 7 months when she was killed.

Tresia had been born and raised in Midland, Texas but moved to Oklahoma City where one of her cousins also resided to start a different life.

In early April, Tresia had decided she needed to go back to Midland to assist her grandmother who had began to have health issues; and to perhaps marry her boyfriend of three years. She had given the credit union her two week notice and was only three days away from leaving Oklahoma City. This was extremely sad for me as I realized she had only been three days away from a new lifetime ahead of her.

The day I found myself grieving for Tresia was the day a relative of mine, living in Midland called to check on how I was doing since the tragedy. I sobbed and told my cousin through tears about Tresia's sad story.

CHRISTY ROSAS

Christy, age 22, was the wife of Chris, mother of Shane, and daughter of Bob and Debbie Pippin.

She was a receptionist at our credit union and was only in her eighth day of employment

We had actively recruited Christy from one of the nearby banks, and she had started her position on April 11, 1995.

I had been on vacation the week of Christy's tenure, and since my return to the office, I had not had the time to even complete her personnel information for our records.

I had made eye contact with this beautiful young lady only a few times. She was the one who told me the printer wasn't working on that fateful morning of April 19th, and she had called the maintenance company and they were on the way to repair it.

I remember Christy addressing me as "Ms. Rogers" and not "Mother Goose" or "Florence" when she told me about the malfunctioning printer which was the greatest indicator that she was a brand new employee.

Christy's information about the printer caused me to move the meeting with the eight staff members to my office instead of the board room where it was originally to take place. This was a big factor in my survival. If the meeting had remained in the board room, I would have perished because that room had been completely annihilated.

No words can describe just how much Christy's death devastated me knowing that we had actually pleaded for her to take the receptionist position.

Since Christy's personnel records hadn't been reported to our insurance company, I initially was informed that she might not even have life insurance or other benefits that we provided to our employees.

However, I made a significant appeal to the insurance company and they ended up paying her benefits to her beneficiaries. I was extremely grateful for their compassion. Christy was one of the last of three bodies removed from the deepest blast impact a month later, and the building had to be imploded before the recovery efforts could continue to search for her remains.

I eventually met Christy's parents at a separate funeral for a mutual friend. I think that must have been the day the tears flowed for Christy as I left the church where the funeral was held, and realized all that her family had lost on that dark day in Oklahoma City.

Christy's lovely mother, Debbie, and I are now Facebook friends and share our sorrow over Christy's loss.

SONJA SANDERS

Sonja Sanders, age 27, was a wife of Mike, mother of Brooklynn and Savanna, daughter of Sheila and Ron Stroud, sister of Kristi Sanders, and native of Moore, Oklahoma.

Sonja was hired January 3, 1989 as a teller in our Operations Department bringing her tenure with the credit union to five years and four months.

Earlier in the chapter, I shared how a phone call with Sonja's mother, Sheila, ensured that I never experienced survivor's guilt. I will never forget it because I was so moved by the act of Sheila's selfless concern for me and the emotional way she conveyed her relief that I had survived while she was yet mourning her daughter's loss.

I have no doubt that Sonja's stellar character was at least in part due to the beautiful mother she had.

My special day of grieving for Sonja is detailed below in the story titled "My Signature Car."

Grieving Stories – My Signature Car

For years, I worked hard in my career and exercised frugality by driving older model cars with several miles on them.

When I finally attained the position of CEO of the Federal Employees Credit Union, it provided a salary that allowed me to invest in what I call my "signature car," so I found myself in a baby blue 1985 Lincoln Town Car.

I really thought I was something driving that big ole beauty.

My parking spot was on the third level of the parking garage underneath the Alfred P. Murrah Federal Building. It was located right next to the door that led to the elevators that took me to my third floor office.

Wow, what a good spot I had!

There were large cement posts on both sides of my car, so it could never be dented by other vehicles.

I happily drove that Lincoln for years until April 19, 1995 when the bomb destroyed the building. After which, I didn't see that car for nearly two weeks.

Early one morning, a young U.S. Marshal, a locksmith, my son Terry, and I met to retrieve my car out of the buildings garage.

There was no electric power, so it was very dark, and the building was in danger of collapsing at any time.

It took the locksmith about 20 minutes to cut a key and bring my car out of the garage.

What a lot of people don't realize about the day of the bombing is that the pipes of the building burst, and it also rained later on that day, so there was significant water damage at the property as well as chemical damage from the bomb.

My once sweet "baby blue" was wet, covered with cement dust, and splattered with ammonia nitrate, an ingredient that Timothy McVeigh included in his homemade bomb.

Once the car was outside of the garage, Terry informed me that he had spoken with my insurance agent. The company had already informed their agents that each of their clients, whose vehicles had been damaged due to the bombing, would be paid the full retail value of those vehicles without question. We were to take the car any place we wanted and have it repaired.

Terry took my car to a small body shop downtown and asked them to clean it up. When they began that arduous task, the entire vinyl top fell apart along with all of the chrome and some of the paint. The acidic and toxic bombing fluids had covered and permanently etched all of the windows beyond repair.

It took 30 days, but the body shop finally got my car repaired to Terry's satisfaction. I really feel like Terry was excited to return my beloved car to me. He has always been such an intuitive son, and he must have known that I needed that "pick me up," and boy did it pick me up! My "baby blue" looked like a brand new car from a showroom floor. Wow, what a great job they had done!

The next day, after I got the car back, I drove from my home to a meeting in downtown Oklahoma City via Western Avenue. The bombing had, of course, destroyed our credit union office space in Oklahoma City, so we had moved to our new location in Bethany, Oklahoma. This meant that it had been weeks since I'd taken the familiar Western Avenue route, but here I was back in my beloved car and taking the route once again.

Over the years, as I took the Western Avenue route to work, I would often pass my head teller, Sonja Sanders, on her way to the office.

Sometimes, we would end up right next to each other at a stoplight. Sonja was a busy mother, so she would frequently take advantage of red lights to apply her makeup and eat her breakfast on the run.

At one light, I would look over, and she would be finishing a donut. At another light, I would look over, and she might be applying her lipstick after wiping the donut crumbs from her lips. (Every woman in that office knew I was a fan of lipstick and having our employees look their best!)

On my way to the meeting, I glanced in my rear view mirror and saw a woman eating a donut.

I cannot explain the wave of emotion that immediately washed over me as I mourned for Sonja and felt the full realization that I would never see her on Western Avenue again.

It was so uncanny how much that lady reminded me of sweet Sonja as she polished off her donut—and on the same street where I had seen Sonja so many mornings! I sobbed so much that I ruined my eye makeup with the tears.

That episode affected me so much that I decided not to drive the Lincoln anymore. I just couldn't! My "signature car" had too many memories.

After my meeting, I drove to our office location in Bethany and told Raymond, my vice president, of the emotional episode I had endured that morning.

I told him I was going to sell that car as soon as I possibly could, and he immediately offered to buy it to accommodate his growing family.

He drove it home that night, and I got back into the rental car that I had been driving since the bombing. I said goodbye to "baby blue" and settled for a great little Buick.

Grieving Stories – Heavenly Geese

In chapter 4, I describe the origin of my initial fascination with geese stemming from my childhood. Years later in the early stages of my career, I realized the powerful comparisons of the flight patterns of geese and corporate leadership. I often applied these principles to my work at various places of employment, and when I became president of the Federal Employees Credit Union, I shared them with my employees who eventually nicknamed me "Mother Goose."

Below is a piece called "Lessons From Geese." It is transcribed from a speech given by Angeles Arrien at the 1991 Organizational Development Network and was based on the work of Milton Olson.

It is a picture of the leadership tenets and geese illustrations I utilized.

1. As each bird flaps its wings, it creates an "uplift" for the bird following. By flying in a "V" formation, the whole flock adds 71% greater flying range than if the bird flew alone.

Lesson: People who share a common direction and sense of community can get where they are going quicker and easier because they are traveling on the thrust of one another.

2. Whenever a goose falls out of formation, it suddenly feels the drag and resistance of trying to fly alone, and quickly gets back into formation to take advantage of the "lifting power" of the bird immediately in front.

Lesson: If we have as much sense as a goose, we will stay in formation with those who are headed where we want to go (and be willing to accept their help as well as give ours to the others).

3. When the lead goose gets tired, it rotates back into the formation and another goose flies at the point position.

Lesson: It pays to take turns doing the hard tasks and sharing leadership—with people, as with geese, we are interdependent on each other.

4. The geese in formation honk from behind to encourage those up front to keep up their speed.

Lesson: We need to make sure our honking from behind is encouraging—
and not something else.

5. When a goose gets sick or wounded or shot down, two geese drop out of formation and follow it down to help and protect it. They stay with it until it is able to fly again or dies. Then they launch out on their own, with another formation, or catch up with the flock.

Lesson: If we have as much sense as geese, we too will stand by each other in difficult times as well as when we are strong.

On May 13, 1995, only a month after the bombing, I addressed a memorial service for my 18 employees of the credit union.

I know that there is a great chasm between this earth and Heaven.

I know that anyone in Heaven is in the Presence of the Lord absent of pain with no feelings of regret, loss, sadness, disappointment, or remorse.

I know that my 18 goslings in Heaven have no memory of that awful bombing as all painful things on earth are passed away. *(Isaiah 25:8; Revelation 21:4)*

I know that God took the sting of death through His Son, Jesus *(1 Corinthians 15:55-57)* and therefore for Believers to be absent in the body is to be present with the Lord. *(2 Corinthians 5:8)*

Regardless of my *knowing* all of this, the very human side of me also *knows* that the splendor of heaven is so amazing that it is beyond our comprehension.

This incomprehensible beauty is also what makes it so difficult for us to understand that our Christian loved ones' absences from this life only means that they've passed on to a place of immeasurable peace. They wouldn't come back to crazy earth even if they had the choice—but that still doesn't mean we don't ascribe earthy attributes to them.

In my address to that memorial service, I attempted to bridge the gap between my imagination, earth's beautiful geese, and what I felt might be Heaven's assignments for my 18 goslings.

MEMO TO MY DEAR LOVELY LADIES FROM THE OLD LEAD GOOSE

I truly don't understand why so many of you had to be taken out of our formation at one time. It is going to be difficult in the days and weeks ahead to keep our meager remaining flock on course as we fly to our destination.

Some of our flock was wounded and will not be able to join our flock for a while. New little ones will take up your places so that we can continue on. The ones who take flight with us will be carefully picked to ensure a safe, successful journey and make you proud so that your legacy will live on.

Today, I can just visualize all you beautiful gals now in your new location in heaven.

Your dedication and enthusiasm has gone with you, and you're probably starting up the "Heavenly Credit Union" where the field of membership is open to all who believe.

Kathy Finley...You are to keep everyone in line so they don't stray too far out of formation.

Claudette...You will continue to have your regular pep rallies, honking loudly to keep up morale, assisting any way you can and continue to serve lots of breakfast casseroles.

Sonja...You will prepare the training sessions so everyone will know their roles and places in line.

Mother Goose

Frankie, Christi, and Tresia... Keep smiling as you did here on earth, instilling confidence and giving of yourself with that personal touch which made everyone feel so special.

Kim Burgess...Make sure things are kept neat and in order, and remember to share with everyone your vivacious nature and positive attitude.

Kathy Leinen and Claudine...The only collecting you will now need to do is new friends, and the only counseling will be with the new arrivals.

Jill...You keep count of the numbers that are arriving and joining your Heavenly Credit Union.

Karan, Coleen, Robbin, and Jamie...You are in a place where money problems no longer exist. You can slow down, relax, rest in the shadow of the Almighty, and let the wind from the others' wings lift you.

Vicki...You will no longer need to worry about credit cards, but instead, perhaps you can issue passes to the streets that are paved with gold.

Virginia and Christy Rosas...You will, no doubt, make sure all new arrivals to the flock of Jesus Christ get to the right place and answer their many questions.

Valerie...You will have a tremendous marketing opportunity ahead of you, and I know you will soar to new heights; but don't forget to keep the details so you can share the history of your days with the rest of the flock when they arrive.

Oh, yes, use Tony Reyes and Linda McKinney to help you get started remembering their dedication and expertise in their roles here on Earth.

Ladies you would be so proud to know how many loved you and how many of your credit union friends (many of whom you have helped from time to time) came to our rescue to ensure our safe recovery for a successful migration.

They flew in from everywhere to assist and gave untiring efforts and did so much in your honor. You'd be so proud.

Your next assignment, ladies, is to help me find a way to thank the many who joined our flight, and don't let me forget to mention the beautiful memorial service given in your honor and to thank the ones who spoke their beautiful words today to your family and friends.

And, oh yes, another item...please remind me to thank all the members that you had spoiled so much; who sent flowers, cards, food, attended your services, cried over your loss, and gave those of us remaining hugs and words of encouragement which gave us the strength to make it through all this turbulence.

Would one of you please take this note for me? And that is, to always keep me cognizant of the needs of the surviving flock: your friends and colleagues, your little credit union family as they mourn your loss from our formation.

I know you are urgently seeking a way to send your loved ones here on Earth an e-mail from your new location. I will volunteer to tell them today what it will say if that's okay with you. I know it would be this:

[2]*Do not stand at my grave and weep,*
I am not there, I do not sleep.
I am a thousand winds that blow,
I am the diamond glints on snow.
I am the sunlight on ripened grain.
I am the gentle autumn rain.
When you awaken in the morning's hush,
I am the swift uplifting rush.
Of quiet birds in circled flight,

---

[2] "Do Not Stand at My Grave and Weep" by Mary Elizabeth Frye (excerpt)

I am the soft stars that shine at night.
Do not stand at my grave and cry,
I am not there. I did not die.

Ladies, do not forget your earthly training. When the lead goose gets tired and has to drop to the back of the formation, take lead and continue on just as you so aptly did here on Earth.

You will be missed so much, but just remember, the old flock will all be together one day, and our worries will be few when we reach our final destination.

Sincerely,
The Old Lead Goose left on Earth to continue the flight
Florence Rogers

Chapter 3
Foreign Territory

A speaking engagement in Australia prepared me for retirement.

I realized that for the majority of my adult life—even when I had kids—I worked. Even when I wasn't pulling a 9-5 and was a "stay at home" mom with my sons, I sold Avon products. If I retired, it would be the first period of my life where I wasn't actively working to generate income and where a group of professionals were not depending on me. I would be left no employees, no co-workers, and no professional obligations.

Even my board memberships and speaking engagements were my choice. That's not the same as a job where you "have" to be there. For the first time, it was just...*me*. I had to deal with *just me*.

On foreign territory in Australia, I realized that my actual life was headed for foreign territory.

To give you a more personal understanding of why the concept of no longer working was such foreign territory for me, I want to take you back to my days at the Federal Employees Credit Union prior to the bombing.

Even "Fun" Was Tied To Work

As I said in chapters 1 and 2, the women on our team were like one big family. While I ran a tight ship, I placed nearly equal importance on interpersonal relationships.

On any team whether professional, family, or friendly, interpersonal associations are important and consequential for unity. Productivity is higher because communication flows more freely. There is less backbiting and intimidation to approach a teammate, and challenges are more readily resolved without conflict.

In addition to celebrating each other's life milestones such as pregnancies, birthdays, and engagements, we also celebrated the holidays—my favorite among which is Christmas.

(You'll see in chapter 5 that I have an entire section dedicated to the festive day!)

For several years prior to the bombing, our staff insisted on holding our office Christmas party in my home, and I was much obliged to host! I mentioned this party in chapter 2 when speaking of my grieving process, but I believe the full story of that party provides good insight on the type of environment I aimed to provide for my employees.

December, 1994 was the final Christmas party with my team prior to the bombing on April, 1995.

Each year, whenever the time for the Christmas party rolled around, I always took the entire day off. The staff was like family, and it felt a bit like I had to clean and prep the house before family came over! Around noon, several of the ladies were allowed to leave work and help me with the food and final preparations for the party.

They felt it was such a privilege to be able to help me with the party that we finally had to have drawings to see who would get to assist me!

The spouses and significant others were never invited to these parties as we just wanted to spend some quality social time together. We usually played "Dirty Santa," enjoyed the food and beverages, and basked in the camaraderie without the stress of the everyday office routine.

This final Christmas party was an event I will never forget. Not only did we have a really great evening with nearly all of the staff present, but there are still reminders throughout my home of that special evening.

While we were enjoying the food and fellowship, a heavy frost was forming outside that we were unaware of, and it was literally covering everything.

Around 11pm, one of the ladies decided she needed to go home to her little family as she had been there since noon helping me set up for the party.

She asked one of her colleagues to move their car from blocking hers so that she could leave. As she backed her car out, it slid on the nearly invisible yet heavy frost, and one of her tires skidded over the small retaining wall that divides my yard from my neighbors' yard.

Everyone panicked. I assured our handful of male employees in attendance that we could, in fact, lift up this employee's car so that she could complete her process of backing out.

"No way, Florence. We can't do that," they replied. "Yes we can," I said.

We did it.

Hearing all of the cheering of our "great accomplishment," Kathy Leinen, one of our collection officers, who had remained inside during all of this, decided to come outside to see what all of the excitement was about.

When Kathy arrived on the scene, unaware of the new sheet of invisible frost, she lost her footing on one of the timbers of that same retaining wall.

She fell into the neighbor's yard and broke her collarbone. Oh no! Not only was she hurt, but she had not yet participated in our annual Christmas champagne toast!

The staff had gifted me a beautiful afghan for Christmas. Victoria Texter, our VISA program manager, quickly grabbed it and wrapped it around Kathy before we took her to the emergency room to protect her from the new blast of cold air that had moved in.

One of the timbers on the top of the retaining wall is still out of place from this episode. It is a constant reminder of the fun night we had, but it also serves as a reminder of how short our lives can be.

Who among us could have known that night would be the last office Christmas party for so many of us? The 18 ladies I lost were such a big part of my life. They were more than employees. They were my family.

The lovely afghan was eventually returned to me when Kathy recovered from her broken collarbone. I find myself remembering that night so often when I enjoy the warmth of that afghan. I keep gifts for a long, long time—some might say, I never get rid of anything that has been given to me. There is still a clock hanging in my home that my employees gifted me along with many other lovely presents they gave me over the years.

My first Christmas after the death of those 18 beautiful women wasn't a joyous one. Even my lifelong love of Christmas could not bring me to enjoy it. After all, December, 1995 was only 8 months after the bombing.

Yes, our office did observe the party again at my home. Yes, we did the champagne tradition again, but that year's toast was a vow that the legacies of those we lost would live on. We smiled as much as we could, but the heaviness in our hearts was starkly juxtaposed to a holiday centered on good cheer.

The tree ornaments we used were ones we had previously used on the office tree year after year. They had been stored in my attic due to lack of office space.

Everything else had been destroyed in the bomb.

18 beautiful handmade ceramic angels also adorned the tree in memory of our colleagues and friends. A sweet lady in West Palm Beach, Florida, who also worked at a credit union, was so moved by our pain as she watched the rescue and recovery coverage on television that she immediately began creating the angels.

It was the last office Christmas party to be held in my home and one that I will never forget, but it was certainly not as special as the one in 1994 that proved to be the last for so many.

Their memories live on in my heart and mind. I will never forget their lovely faces and will always treasure the mementos they left behind.

That's the kind of environment I fostered at the FECU. An environment of love. It was one of several reasons why my eventual decision to retire was not an easy one to come by.

Misogyny

Another factor in deciding whether or not to retire also had to do with just how much I had overcome to be an effective CEO. I was, quite frankly, proud to have made so many leaps and bounds—many of which I dealt with internally. Was I really ready to give up all of that ahead of what could have been three or four more years of real progress?

At the root of those leaps and bounds was misogyny.

I had always dealt with some measure of misogyny as the CEO of a financial institution, but none of it seemed as prevalent as the misogyny I faced after the bombing.

I guess because, no matter what sexist comments or situations I may have found myself in prior to the bombing, none of them prevented me from actually doing my job.

Boys Club Prior To The Bombing

My generation of women entered the workforce in the 1950's, and many of us had been inspired by the iconic Rosie the Riveter media character of the 1940's which represented women pulling an equal share of the workforce weight during World War II.

However, even with this representation of progress, many of us felt we had one of three options in the workplace: 1.) accept positions in a limited pool nearly always regulated to the bottom of the salary barrel 2.) work very hard to attain a senior position but endure the comments and consistent reduction of our importance down to our body parts in order to "play the boys game" by laughing off their comments and/or advances.

In my career, I found myself laughing off a lot of comments and cleverly maneuvering out of compromising situations where I was hit on.

During my tenure at FECU, I was one of a handful of women CEOs at Oklahoma City-based credit unions. I believe there were three at the time, and I formed a close relationship with one of them.

She and I often ended up on business trips together because our credit unions were frequently invited to the same conferences.

Among the several (not all) of the remaining CEOs who were all male, my friend and I were given the nicknames: "big boobs" and "cute butt."

I was "cute butt."

Present-day women in the workplace may read this and clutch their pearls in disgust, but truthfully, the environment was so male-dominated that at the time, I personally didn't necessarily take offense to it choosing instead to make shoot jocular jokes back at the men.

Right or wrong, it was "just the way it was," and the men seemed to enjoy my company. I am not sure if my friend took personal offense or not, but she had a similar response and also chose to joke back with the men.

However, as I think back on this, I realize that I was probably not as bothered by the comments for two reasons: 1.) they did not actually affect my ability to do my job 2.) they did not serve as a deciding factor of whether or not I ascended to the top of my field.

I was the CEO, and the sexually charged comments leveraged at me by other male CEOs in my field were not going to change that.

Not everyone was is the position I was in, though, and that is where the bigger problems come in.

Let me be clear.

No woman, whether she is a CEO or the office custodian, should ever be subjected to objectification in the work place, but where the recent rise of the equality movement gained more legs is when it became blatantly evident that women's advancement in the workplace was directly being impacted by a number of men who were abusing their positions of power.

When a woman is reduced to her body parts and not allowed to succeed without sleeping with someone or without having inappropriate comments leveraged at her so that her male superiors or counterparts "feel that there is a possibility that they could sleep with her" a toxic environment is created, and that is never okay.

It really is a shame looking back on these times that those names were tolerated, but my sense of humor always seemed to get me through it, and, at the time, I wasn't truly bothered by it.

I concluded that's "the way it was" and chose survival mode instead. I even once cracked a joke about it in a speech honoring my friend, the other female CEO at her retirement celebration letting everyone know that at my age, my butt was neither little nor cute anymore.

Again, while I had a quick wit, I want to reiterate that no one—man or woman—should be put in a position to either "tolerate" inappropriate behavior or face professional consequences.

Not everyone is able to brush off harassment with a joke or flippant comment.

For the sake of privacy, I've elected not to share other experiences where a humorous quip wasn't enough to clear me from compromising situation's but I do want the readers to know that I endured them, and I can empathize with others who have.

There is no room in humanity for emotional or physical abuse of power. We are all valuable beings made in the image of God. We should be treated as such and treat others as such.

Misogyny After The Bombing

On top of battling grief, enduring injuries, and helming a rebuild of our decimated credit union, I also faced multiple clashes with a number of the FECU board members who questioned the ability of a woman in her 60s to continue in my position of leadership under such grueling circumstances.

Despite the success I'd had in growing the credit union to new heights, they still doubted my abilities. Yes, the bombing presented several circumstances that none of us could have predicted, but had I not proven my competence after all these years? It was as if my hard work and highest points in my career had not built any credit, and I could not get a loan of confidence.

After my neck surgery for relief from my bombing-related injuries, I showed up to work in my neck brace still performing at a high level including regular meetings with the board as we navigated our rebuilding process, and not a single one of them asked how I was doing or offered any sort of moral support. On top of questioning my abilities, this seeming lack of empathy was a double-blow. I had put so much effort into fostering personal relationships with employees, credit union members, and board members, so to get this kind of response really hurt.

I never complained. I didn't even miss work other than a few days with the surgery—and even that was months after the bombing, not immediately after the bombing. I jumped right in leading the way and working unseemly hours to ensure our members that their accounts were intact.

Yet, I couldn't even get a simple: "Hey, Florence, how are you holding up? I couldn't imagine losing 18 employees. How is your neck? It must be so uncomfortable for you. Let us know if you need anything."

My kids were grown, and I was divorced at the time. While my friends and family regularly checked up on me, my empty home (save my dog) would frequently feel like a cavernous space exacerbating my loneliness as I battled grief and felt like the board members of the institution where I had poured in so much of my heart were not returning the love.

Perhaps what bothered me most was the eventual salary battle. Nothing shows an employee how much they are appreciated than their salary.

Money talks, and I was literally shocked at how much I had to fight just to be paid according to the GS scale for my position and length of tenure as the CEO of the Federal Employees Credit Union.

For those who are unfamiliar with the GS scale, here is an explanation from the U.S. Office of Personnel Management (OPM).

The OPM serves as the chief human resources agency and personnel policy manager for the Federal Government. The General Schedule (GS) classification and pay system covers the majority of civilian white-collar Federal employees (about 1.5 million worldwide) in professional, technical, administrative, and clerical positions. GS classification standards, qualifications, pay structure, and related human resources policies (e.g., general staffing and pay administration policies) are administered by the U.S. Office of Personnel Management (OPM) on a Government-wide basis.

Each agency classifies its GS positions and appoints and pays its GS employees filling those positions following statutory and OPM guidelines.

The General Schedule has 15 grades--GS-1 (lowest) to GS-15 (highest). Agencies establish (classify) the grade of each job based on the level of difficulty, responsibility, and qualifications required. Individuals with a high school diploma and no additional experience typically qualify for GS-2 positions; those with a Bachelor's degree for GS-5 positions; and those with a Master's degree for GS-9 positions.

Each grade has 10 step rates (steps 1-10) that are each worth approximately 3 percent of the employee's salary. Within-grade step increases are based on an acceptable level of performance and longevity[3]

Not only did I advocate for a raise in my own salary, but for the salaries of my employees as well.

[3] OPM.gov, "Policy, Data, Oversight PAY & LEAVE"

I referenced the GS scale as the basis for my argument when requesting that my employees were paid the appropriate salaries and also that their salaries would be matched with credit union funds to make up for what workers compensation insurance did not cover.

In Spite Of The Misogyny

In spite of the misogyny and with no college degree, “this ol’ gal from Minco” still managed to rack up an impressive stack of accomplishments. Even in my 80s, as I write this, I smile in humble astonishment that a woman who grew up in a home with no electricity was able to do these things. I’m still just a girl from rural Oklahoma! Here’s the list.

- Elected as the first woman Board Chairman of the Oklahoma Credit Union League in 1993.
- Inducted into the CUES Hall of Fame in 1995. Success Magazine wrote a nice feature (also mentioned in chapter 1)
- Voted Oklahoma’s Professional of the Year in 1997
- Inducted into the Cornerstone Credit Union League Hall of Fame along with a Citation of Honor as a Distinguished Oklahoma Recipient from the State of Oklahoma in 2016

Here is an article published in a 1995 edition of Success Magazine.

"Rogers Inducted Into 1995 CUES Hall of Fame"

This is the last in a series of profiles about the 1995 Hall of Fame Inductees.

When credit union leaders think of someone who's truly helped a credit union through tough times, Florence Rogers comes to mind.

Rogers, president/CEO of $77 million Federal Employees Credit Union, was among the survivors of the April 19, 1995 bombing of the Alfred P. Murrah Federal Building in Oklahoma City.

The blast took the lives of 18 FECU employees and destroyed the credit union's facility.

Within hours of the blast, Rogers and other surviving staffers met and made plans for getting the credit union back up and running for its 15,000 members. Today, "normal" operations take place in an Oklahoma City suburb, Bethany, Oklahoma, but the past is not forgotten.

Rogers was inducted into the 1995 CUES Hall of Fame at CUES' CEO Network '95 last October in Ponte Vedra Beach, FL, not just for her dedication in a time of crises, but also for her long-term contributions to credit unions and her community.

A member of CUES since 1973, Rogers regularly has attended CUES' Annual Convention & Exposition and its members-only CEO Network conferences. She attended CUES Strategic Marketing Conference in 1991.

She's been active in the Oklahoma Credit Union League, serving as its first female chairman in 1993. She was a national director for the Credit Union National Association from 1988 to 1994.

In her community, Rogers has been active in the Black Program Council, an educational program to further African-Americans in the federal employment system and in the Christian Women's Fellowship Organization.

A special edition of Newsweek Magazine focused on my unique story.

Jack Querry, The Man Who Stood By Me

The 18th President of the United States, Ulysses S. Grant once said: *"The friend of my adversity I shall always cherish most. I can better trust those who helped to relieve the gloom of my dark hours than those who are so ready to enjoy with me the sunshine of my prosperity."*

Having served as a Commanding General of the U.S. Army during the most divided time in American history and having served as President through the 1873 economic depression, Grant delivered this statement with authority as he was much acquainted with controversy.

I've had many friends, but Jack Querry's friendship was an embodiment of Grant's words.

Jack Querry was serving as Board Chairman of the FECU when the bombing happened. He had held an FECU board member position since 1979 and faithfully served it until his death on December 7, 2018.

I really admired Jack as a quality individual. Not only was he a pleasant person to be around, but his professional resume was quite impressive. After his military service with the United States Army and graduation from the University of Oklahoma College of Law, he began a 28-year career of dedicated service with the Criminal Investigation Division of the Internal Revenue Service, so he brought a unique set of skills to the credit union board, and I really cannot think of anyone who could have better served us as our chairman.

One of Jack's strongest and most useful attributes was his incredible memory. In fact, it was so good that it might have been photographic. After the bombing, I realized just how valuable his memory was in two areas:

1. ***The Binder*** - On the very afternoon of the bombing, Jack called an emergency board meeting to discuss the future of the credit union with our members' accounts and employees at the forefront of his mind. Jack had faithfully kept a large binder at his home that contained all of the policies and regulations that affected the credit union. He had internalized so much of that data that he was able to navigate that meeting with ease. As post-bombing credit union policy changes occurred, Jack was furnished with new copies and was able to help us quickly navigate the new territory having been able to quickly note the differences between the old and new policies. Jack's binder was vital in the reestablishment of Federal Employees Credit Union, and, looking back on this, I really don't know how we would have been able to

pull the credit union back together without *it* or without *him*.

2. ***Remembering My Track Record*** – Major life events such as tragedies, increased wealth, or attaining fame truly reveal a person's character. They usually either fold or thrive under pressure, and very quickly, their selflessness, loyalty, sound decision making and/or lack thereof becomes evident very quickly. If I was the "Stalwart Woman," as my sons had labeled me, then Jack was the "Resolute Man." He provided the leadership and grace under fire that our board needed.

   With our city smothered in bombing recovery efforts and our credit union decimated from tragedy, several of the seven board members expressed concerns to Jack that they were concerned that I could not handle the task of putting the credit union back in business. "Why don't we allow Tinker Federal Credit Union absorb it into their membership," they suggested.

   In true leadership fashion, Jack knew to bring the temperature down. He remembered the work that I had put in prior to the bombing leading the credit union to its largest revenue in its history, and he insisted to the other board members that they should not hurriedly dismiss either me or the possibility of a regenerated credit union.

Jack's knowledge of the credit union and his belief that I could handle the huge tasks ahead worked in successful synchronization to ultimately reopen the credit union for business in 48 hours and 18 minutes after the bombing occurred.

I wore a tough emotional exterior, but had I not had the support of Jack Querry, I might have folded under pressure, and I am forever grateful to him.

Jack and I remained in touch after my retirement in 1997 and exchanged birthday greetings every year. I miss our phone visits and I think he would agree that *Mother Goose* is the perfect title for this book.

The Defining Moment. My Retirement Decision

Hopefully, now you can see that after having spent so many years working, so many years on my toes, so many years working in craft I love, so many years proving over and over again that I was "good enough" to run with the industry's most important men...the thought of having to leave was—a lot.

What's interesting is that while I eventually retired from a specific 9 to 5, I never really stopped working. It was just in a different capacity.

After retirement, I still remained involved with the Oklahoma City National Memorial and Museum, my neighborhood association, the Cleveland County Election Board, my church, and my family's lively reunions!

However, as I've stated, there was still a defining moment when I finally realized it was time to hang up the credit union cleats and leave the financial industry football field. I had run my last financial touchdown.

I was on my way back home from Australia where I had been invited for a speaking engagement, and there was something about that return flight home that enabled me to think. It was the type of deep thinking that allowed me to be both introspective about my life and my emotions as well as observant of my external circumstances.

I realized that as much as I loved the people and the actual aspects of my job, the stress of my battles with the board were really starting to wear on me.

As a woman in her early sixties, I was far from the rocking chair, but I no longer wanted to expend the physical nor mental energy to fight those battles when I knew in my heart that I had won the war. I'd had a good career. I'd survived a bomb and brought the credit union back after the destruction from it.

Now, I would move into a different phase of life.

It was time for me to retire—not retire from being effective on behalf of various causes that I believed in—not retired from life—but retired from the 9 to 5 daily work grind.

For the youngsters reading this, understand that once you've reached a certain level of maturity—whether that be at age 40 or age 60—you will eventually reach a point where your "give a crapper" wears out. Your "give a crapper" will no longer crank up no matter how many times you push the starter button or turn the key, and you will not want to give anymore of your time to things that are not significant.

Were the credit union members and employees significant?

Yes.

Were the petty fights with the board members?

No—especially when I had earned the right to be trusted, and some of them treated me otherwise.

One of the most memorable examples happened when my out-of-state speaking engagements began to increase, and it really hit home with me during a visit to Australia.

As I enjoyed the beautiful landscape of Albury, Australia with its botanical gardens and beautiful boasting mountains, along the continent's longest river, The Murray, I reflected on the two speeches that I would soon deliver as the keynote speaker for the Australia Credit Unions.

On top of recounting my experience with the bombing and speaking of our FECU rebuild, I would be sure to include my appreciation for their multi-faceted support. After the bombing, approximately $1.6M had been contributed to the FECU from credit unions throughout the United States, Canada, and Australia—an outpouring I could not have previously fathomed even if I had tried.

I was so grateful for their generosity toward our FECU family. I couldn't believe that I was almost prevented from attending due to some of our board members' obstinacy and suspicions.

I was grateful for all of it, but to receive contributions from Canada and Australia really touched me. I was humbled and honored that our institution was on the hearts and minds of people in other countries and on a whole other continent! Because of this, I gladly accepted speaking engagement requests in Canada and Australia. However, I never took a dime of honorarium speaking fees. Instead, I redirected each of those contributions—even the ones that came directly to the FECU—to:

1. The Oklahoma City Memorial Foundation towards the creation of the Oklahoma City National Memorial & Museum
2. FECU deceased victims' families
3. Injured survivors, and any FECU survivors who were impacted by the bombing.

None of this stopped several of the FECU board members from questioning me about the trips to Canada and Australia.

They accused me of using company time for personal gain. I was really taken aback by it, but looking back on this with a 20/20 lens, I believe that they were just jealous of me.

Jealousy makes people look and sound very unintelligent because they are projecting their insecurities onto their target while their target is usually just being themselves or has their mind in another place entirely. It reminds me of their comments: "My wife doesn't make that much!"

On the way home from Australia, my decision was made. It was time to let go of the job I had loved with all of my heart. I had given it my time, my soul, and my strength.

A new chapter was on the horizon, and I was at peace with that.

Be Prepared

I am a good saver. It's a trait I've had all of my life, and it definitely came in handy from my 60s until the present.

I had no pension at the credit union, and I convinced the board to fund it to its appropriate level after the bombing. I saw that the end of my tenure was near, and I knew that pension would have to see me through. Since I ended up only staying two years after the bombing, my pension was funded at two years' worth.

An intelligent and insightful investment counselor who actually worked at another credit union shared sound financial advice with me. Therefore, I was able to stretch and flip those two years' worth of pension into more funds and for a longer time.

I would scream these next sentences from a mountaintop if I thought every working professional could hear me: Make plans to save and grow your money, now. Don't wait until you're in your 60s to start thinking about retirement. One day you'll lie down 37 and wake up 62. Your career goes by very quickly.

Be prepared.

A Gracious Exit And A Building Dedicated In My Honor

Always be as gracious as you can when leaving a place. It will leave a lasting impression, and even if things aren't as pleasant as you would like for them to be.

Looking back, I'm very happy that I left in a manner that I felt was classy and that I held my dignity rather than rolling in the "mud" with my naysayers.

Focusing on the positive is so much more powerful than dwelling on the negative. It communicates the strong elements of a legacy to inspire those coming behind you to give their best.

In the final "President's Message" article of our monthly credit union newsletter, these were my parting words:

Two years ago, I was faced with the most difficult task of my 26-year career with FECU. That challenge was leading the Credit Union back into existence and hiring competent staff quickly and efficiently that could carry our legacy long into the 21st century.

I cannot, however, take all the credit for our miraculous recovery. Surviving staff members, volunteers from many credit unions, as well as our credit union friends across the nation, Canada, and Australia all rallied with offers of assistance and generous contributions for the victims' families and survivors. Our gratitude to them can never be adequately expressed in words.

Now, two years since the tragedy, I feel the task of re-establishing the Credit Union has been accomplished. I can now announce my plans to retire in June and know that I am leaving the Credit Union in good hands.

I am currently serving on the Board of the Oklahoma City Memorial Foundation as well as some of the committees involved with the permanent memorial planned for the Murrah Building site and will volunteer some time to that organization. I will also stay involved with the building project for the new offices planned for FECU.

I know I will miss the daily routines, as well as many of my favorite members whom I have known so many years, but I have decided it is time to "do something for Florence."

These past two years have been long and sometimes stressful as we dealt daily with unfamiliar issues. We did, however, achieve a long time goal of mine, which was to be rated a 5-star credit union in 1996.

I was deeply touched at our 34th Annual Meeting, as each staff member presented me with a long stem red rose and the following words on a beautiful plaque:

> ***With your leadership and under your wing, we have learned to fly.***
> ***With your wisdom and guidance, we have the skills to rise to new heights.***
> ***With your knowledge given to us, we have the strength to soar to the future.***
> ***You have earned our respect & love, & you will always be our Mother Goose.***
> ***--Your Loving Flock of FECU***
> ***March 15, 1997***

It is my prayer, as I drop out of the formation, that FECU will continue to prosper and continue to consider member service, the highest priority. My sincere thanks to you, the members, who have made my career with Federal Employees Credit Union a joyous one.

A couple of years later, I was invited to the ribbon cutting ceremony for the opening of the new FECU headquarters when they moved to a different location. A building was dedicated to me, and it was one of the most significant honors of my life.

I am so glad that despite some of the issues I endured toward the end of my tenure, I left on a positive note, and my parting words were sweet.

"Sticking it to" the board or throwing passive aggressive shots at them on my way out would not have been worth it, and, as I stood there looking at my dedication plaque, those board members and their antics seemed less and less significant.

Unforgettable Trip to Kenya

My early retirement at age 62 marked the first time ever in my adult life that I wasn't doing anything at all to make a living—even dating back to when I was 18 years old!

It was foreign territory, but how grateful I was that three years later in the year 2000, I was freed up to explore a different foreign territory on another continent.

Had I still been working, I either might not have been available for this trip, or I might not have been able to enjoy it as much without the distractions or stresses of the FECU responsibilities waiting for me back home.

A group of people out of Harrisonburg, VA calling themselves "peacemakers" arranged a cultural exchange between survivors and victims' family members of the Oklahoma City Bombing and survivors and victims' family members of United States Embassy bombings in Africa. I was invited as a member of the Oklahoma City delegation.

Though the embassy bombings occurred in both Tanzania and Kenya, our exchange took place in Kenya.

Since the Oklahoma City Bombing occurred in 1995 and the embassy bombings happened in 1998, the peacemakers thought that we would have a lot in common.

It is always amazing to me that among victims or survivors of tragedy, racism tends to take a backseat. No one is concerned about anyone's color or ethnicity. You are bound together by your humanity. I saw this with the Oklahoma City Bombing, these embassy bombings, and later with the September 11th attacks of 2001.

This trip was an incredibly special turning point in which I experienced a deeper level of healing than I even knew I needed.

Here is a large excerpt from an article about the exchange published in Harrisonburg's Daily News Record Newspaper.

Time to Heal: Oklahoma survivors and family members visit Nairobi, Kenya in 2000

Local Peacemakers Unite Victims of Oklahoma, Nairobi Bombings

Article in the Daily News Record Harrisonburg, VA — Saturday July 15, 2000

"The pain was the same—the grief for lost loved ones, the scars and the trauma. Survivors of the bombings in Oklahoma City and the U.S. Embassy in Nairobi, Kenya, found they had much in common as they met with each other and a number of Harrisonburg peacemakers, who organized the exchange program."

"As they started sharing stories, people would say. "If I couldn't see you talking, I couldn't tell whether you were from Nairobi or Oklahoma City because our stories are pretty much the same: says Jan Jenner who works for the Conflict Transformation Program at Eastern Mennonite University.

Jenner, along with a student and a professor organized two week-long sessions-first with six Kenyan survivors in Oklahoma City, then with four Oklahomans and hundreds of Kenyans in Nairobi. These healing workshops and the discussions and visits to bomb sites and memorials allowed the participants to share their experiences with each other.

Many of the survivors of both bombings sometimes found that their experiences were very similar. Jenner said she saw amazing changes throughout the two weeks.

The Oklahomans who participated in this exchange were Florence Rogers, a survivor of the Oklahoma City bombing in 1995, along with Susan Urbach, also a survivor, "Bud" Welch, who lost his daughter, Julie, in the bombing, and

Frank Silovsky, a widower whose wife had died soon after the Oklahoma bombing.

The Nairobi terrorist bomb attack on the US Embassy took the lives of 218 and injured several thousand others. The date was August 7, 1998.

The Kenyans had never organized a family/survivor group, so it was something those from Oklahoma City and Harrisonburg,VA were going to assist with...

I penned this personal account of the trip not long after returning to the United States.

"The four of us from Oklahoma City flew to Nairobi on the 4th of July, 2000 on American Airlines to London where we had a very long layover before connecting to the British Airways and on to Kenya.

We were met at the airport in Nairobi by a small group of the Kenyans, even some that we had remembered from their recent visit to Oklahoma City. Everyone was so excited to see each other. A small bus took us to the Fairview Hotel where we would spend the next week. The Hotel was a beautiful red brick building surrounded by 5 acres of luxuriant tranquil gardens and was the main hotel that was used for business travelers.

Little did we "okies" know when we checked in that we were to experience many different customs that were unexpected and unknown to us. I shared a hotel room with Susan Urbach. Frank and Bud also shared a room. We couldn't wait to see more of Nairobi. It was dark when we arrived since there is only one flight in at night and one flight out. The flight out is at 10:30 p.m. which is the one we left on.

It was winter in Nairobi and we saw the Kenyans arriving at our meetings with coats, gloves, and earmuffs on some even wearing two pair of pants. We loved the temperatures that were only about 70 degrees. We showed up in shirt sleeves enjoying the cool weather since we had left Oklahoma's hot July weather.

There were no screens on the windows, but there were curtains that wrapped around the beds at night to keep the mosquitoes and flies away. Our rooms were quite lovely even if they weren't anything like the US hotels we had been accustomed to in our travels.

We enjoyed wonderful breakfast buffets every morning where some of the food items we didn't recognize, but were wonderful anyway. The Kenyans met us early every morning to enjoy the breakfasts and were so anxious to get acquainted with us and attend the planned meetings. Many of them had arrived by taxis or busses, but many of them had walked several miles from their homes to the hotel. The Kenyans weren't really "huggers" like the Oklahomans, but before we left, all of that had changed. They were so charming. We sometimes had a little difficulty understanding their formal English. I'm sure we sounded pretty strange to them when we talked.

The meetings would start fairly early every day, then lunch, then some really neat excursions when we adjourned. The Kenyans had never told their stories of survival or loss of their loved ones, but about the second day, they began to open up and tell their stories of loss. There were tears at times from those in attendance, including the Oklahoma guests. We certainly knew the impacts of their sorrow and could relate to their grief. They would show up with special meaning items of their loved ones who had died. One widower brought his wife's shoes that she had been wearing when she was killed, and the list is long as they told their stories. As each day of the meetings ended, we could see and feel the impact we had created with our new Kenyan friends.

One evening we attended a lovely meal in one of the survivor's homes. USAID sponsored several such meals in the homes assisting with the meal costs. Small peanuts and beer appeared in all of the host homes that were a huge luxury for the Kenyans and a treat for us also. We were met with gratitude from the officers and staff of USAID representatives. The homes where we met were considered middle class Kenyans. We found ourselves counting our blessings back in the US. Some of the homes had no washers or dryers, or even refrigerators. You could see the excitement when bags of ice showed up for the evenings.

We enjoyed a shopping trip one afternoon where we purchased fabrics, and souvenirs to bring home.

We were excited for the Safari to the Nairobi National Park where we saw all of the big 5 animals and many, many more. I felt like we were on a trip with National Geographic. One day we took a bus far into the desert where we saw a small building ahead of us. The only plants or trees around this building were a few small Umbrella Thorn (Acacia tortillis) trees that required little water. I was fascinated with the little thorns from the trees and I have to confess that I took one of the little thorns that had fallen from one of the trees and tucked it away in my luggage and brought it back to Oklahoma along with a little rock from the desert. About a month after returning home, I was looking through a little pile of the souvenirs with plans to move them from my dining room table. I was shocked to see a tiny live black ant crawl out of a tiny hole in the thorn. I was literally amazed that he had survived that long journey all the way to the U.S.

We saw many of the Maasai women walking with buckets on their heads making their way to the small building where they worked and made beautiful bead products entirely by hand. The buckets they brought were filled with water when they left their shifts, so they could take water to their families. This was their place of employment that earned them a small salary. We later learned that the proper name was Utamaduni Crafts Centre.

The week literally flew by and it was time to say our goodbyes to our wonderful Kenyan friends.

Jan Jenner, who had organized the exchange, had lived in Nairobi for eight years while her husband served as a missionary, so she was saying goodbye to many of her friends from those years. She told the newspaper reporter that it was her hope that the Nairobi and Oklahoma City survivors would keep their relationships going, and that came true. We have kept in touch through the years since with email and Facebook. We learned that one of the young widows, mother of two young sons, died a few years ago with a massive heart attack, leaving the two sons who were now in their late teen years. She had been one of the hostesses who entertained us in her home one evening. We were saddened to learn of her unexpected death.

We left Nairobi and said goodbye to our new Kenyan friends the 11th of July. Many of the Kenyans had walked many miles just to see us leave at 10:30 at night. They brought gifts for all of us and were so sad to see us leave, and yes, there were many hugs for everyone. Some of the gifts were difficult to manage through the airports since our luggage had already been loaded, but we so appreciated their love offerings. I still have several of those gifts in my home with the fond memories of a very special journey to the beautiful country of Africa.

Public Speaking: The OTHER Foreign Territory

I'm again going to jump backwards a bit from the Kenya story and the foreign territory of my retirement to speak about another very important foreign territory of my life: professional public speaking.

After the bombing, I was suddenly presented with opportunities to speak extensively throughout the United States.

I even accepted invites to Canada, Australia, and, of course, Kenya telling my story of survival and giving disaster recovery presentations.

In chapter 4, you will see that I definitely wasn't a shy child or teenager. I even graduated as valedictorian of my high school class and had to deliver a public graduation speech, but professional public speaking is a horse of a different color—a much different color than the horse I rode to school down those country Minco, Oklahoma roads.

After the bombing, not only was I in high demand to tell my story, but I was in high demand to offer some type of insight. Requested topics ranged from rebuilding the credit union to recovery from injuries to my grieving process, and it was...*a lot.*

The majority of my life's learning experiences occurred by me just "doing" or just being "thrown into the middle" of something, and I figured it out. It was a lifelong method of survival if you will, and this type of professional public speaking was no different.

On April 19, 1995 at 9:01am, I was "Florence Rogers, CEO of the Federal Employees Credit Union." One minute later at 9:02am, I was a bombing survivor, and my life hasn't been the same since.

Suddenly, I was some type of authority (a *speaking* authority) on the aforementioned topics, and I did the only thing I knew how to do: square my shoulders back, fight tears as best I could, tell the truth, and just get through it.

Ultimately, I believe this worked because it was authentic. I didn't have any formal public speaking training. I just told audiences the play-by-play of what happened before, during, and after the bombing and how I didn't have much time for reflection. I had to move quickly, and the grieving process wove its way through nearly every aspect of my rebuilding activities.

I have delivered so many speeches that there is no way I could possibly fit them all into this book, but I did include a list of speaking engagements in the 5 years after the bombing (1995-2000).

Looking back on this list as I write this in my 80's, I marvel at the energy I had and wonder: "Who was that gal, and where did she get all of that strength?"

A scripture comes to mind: Psalm 121: 1-8.

[1] I will lift up mine eyes unto the hills, from whence cometh my help.
[2] My help cometh from the LORD, which made heaven and earth.
[3] He will not suffer thy foot to be moved: He that keepeth thee will not slumber.
[4] Behold, He that keepeth Israel shall neither slumber nor sleep.
[5] The LORD is thy keeper: the LORD is thy shade upon thy right hand.
[6] The sun shall not smite thee by day, nor the moon by night.
[7] The LORD shall preserve thee from all evil: He shall preserve thy soul.
[8] The LORD shall preserve thy going out and thy coming in from this time forth, and even for evermore.

Yes, that was it. It had to be God—a supernatural strength. The burdens of hiring replacements for 18 dead employees; operating in a temporary location while rebuilding a bombed out business; ensuring our clients that their records and accounts would be intact;

working through physical pain; and becoming a public figure was not something I could have done on my own.

Couple that with the fact that those girls were actually my friends. They were like daughters and sisters to me, and there was no way to authentically separate my personal feelings from the situation. I had been their Mother Goose, and they had been my goslings. I was grieving my friends silently, and I grieved each time I held one of their loved ones in a long embrace and shared a memory or returned a concrete dust-covered or blood-stained belonging to one of them.

It was God. It was definitely God. I'm no superwoman, but I was indeed granted supernatural strength.

Here's that list I promised you.

Speaking Engagements and Trips post the Oklahoma City Bombing

June, 1995..........Nashville, TN (inducted into the Credit Union Executive Society's Hall of Fame)
Gave a short presentation to approximately 2000 Credit Union Leaders from across the US.

June 1995 Palm Springs, CA (was on program about Disaster Recovery) presented to Credit Union CEO organization along with Bill Towler, our disaster recovery company in Oklahoma City, OK. Approximately 200 companies represented.

July 9-12 Savannah, GA Georgia Credit Union League and Affiliates Annual Meeting.

August 17th NARFE in Oklahoma City, OK. (National Association Retired Federal Employees

October 14-18 Ponte Verda Beach, Jacksonville, FL. Credit Union Executives Society annual CEO Network conference. Approximately 300 Credit Unions represented.

October 19th Oklahoma City, Bank Administration Institute meeting at Marriott ;200 attendees.

October 26th Dallas, TX CUNA Annual Meeting. I was a delegate for Oklahoma Credit Unions.

Nov. 16th San Francisco, CA spoke to the Disaster Preparedness Informational Council of CA. App. 400 to 500 companies represented.

Dec 1st Dallas, TX (Dallas Postal Credit Union dedicated a new branch office to the lost FECU

Employees and I was a speaker at the dedication ceremony.)

Dec 5th San Francisco, CA speaker at Chevron Federal Credit union.

1996 speaking engagements.

March 20-22 Seattle, WA guest speaker at a credit union workshop on disaster recovery. App 300 .

March 28-Apr 1 Toronto, Canada guest speaker at annual meeting of Credit Unions in Canada. App 80 in attendance.

May 16-19 Pittsburg, PA. Credit Unions in PA annual meeting. Keynote speaker at their kick-off Luncheon for their Foundation. App. 1500 present.

June 28-30 Rochester, NY Annual Meeting of NY Credit Unions. App 900 in attendance.

August 24-27 Panama City, FL (speaker at Gulf Coast Regulatory Conference. Credit Unions from FL and GA in attendance. App 200.

Sept 6-8 Park City, Utah speaker for Utah Credit Unions. App. 300

Nov. 13-16 Anaheim, CA California Credit Union League Annual Meeting; Barbara Bush was a speaker also. Appl 1500 to 2000 in attendance. Held at Disney Land Hotel.

1997 TRIPS AND SPEECHES

Feb 17-March 4 Albury, Australia. Trip sponsored by Cuna Mutual Branch in Sydney. Keynote speaker Australia Credit Unions held in Albury App. 700 in attendance. Did 2 speeches. One on disaster recovery and another on FECU story.

May 29-June 1 Grand Rapids, MI to speak at the Michigan Credit Union Leagues Annual Meeting. Over 1000 in attendance.

May Denver, CO. Made several trips to Denver to testify in McVeigh trial.

Sept 7th Boston, MA. Guest speaker at meeting for Operations officers of Credit Unions. Sponsored by EasCorp in Woburn MA.

Oct 23-26 Vancouver, BC. Guest speaker for Canadian Credit Unions and Insurance Institute of BC This was a terrorism workshop)

Nov 18-21 Point Clear, AL. Guest speaker for credit Union leaders from Alabama and Mississippi. App. 300 in attendance.

1998 SPEAKING TRIPS AND SPEECHES

March 25th Oklahoma City, Speech at Reserve National Life Insurance Co.

March 31st Oklahoma City, Spoke for Weokie Credit Union (Spirit of Cooperation theme)

April 23rd Columbus, Ohio. Keynote Speaker for Ohio Credit Union Leagues Annual Meeting # 64

May 1st Jackson, MS. Speaker for Mississippi Credit Union System.

Sept 1st Calumet High School in Calumet , OK

Sept 2nd Chisolm Trail Vo-Tech in Oklahoma City

September Ocean City, MD Terrorism Workshop accompanied by Chief Marrs and Billl Johnson froı OK.

1999 TRIPS AND SPEECHES

Feb 11th Yukon, OK. Speech at the Yukon Library.

June 24th Orlando, FL. Trip sponsored by Nearman CPA and Associates.

Sept 21-25 Baltimore, MD. Terrorism Conference in Ocean City, MD for FBI

Oct 15th Oklahoma City, U.S. Marshalls Annual Meeting at Marriott.

2000 TRIPS AND SPEECHES

July 4-11 Nairobi, Kenya Meeting with widows and survivors after their US Embassy bombing ,in 1998 to assist with organizing a memorial for the 218 who died and several thousand

	injured.This trip was sponsored by Eastern Nazarene University and U.S. Aid. Four Oklahoma City, OK were myself, Bud Welch, Susan Urbach and Frank Silovsky.Sev from the University were there also.
July 29th 2000	Gulfport, MS. Speaker for MS Credit Union System. Survivor Story Speech. Second day gave speech for their Audit Committee.
April 2001	New Haven, CT United Shoreline Credit Union Chapter Meeting.
April 2001	Oklahoma City, OK Retired State Employees
June, 2001	New Haven CT. United Shoreline Credit Union Chapter meeting.
June 2002	New Orleans, LA (Took grandson on this one)
Jan 8, 2003	Enid, OK speech for ONG employees association
Aug 13, 2004	Defense Attorney Workshop
Sept 2006	LA, Louisiana Credit Union League
March 2009	DAR in Edmond
Sept 2010	Oklahoma City, OK ATT Pioneers
May 2011	Oklahoma child Care of Oklahoma City, OK
Sept 19th, 2012	OKC Memorial. Speech to Teachers on the Financial Impact the bombing had on C
May 2014	Oklahoma City National Memorial Speech for graduating seniors' from Southeast School. About 100 Seniors.
April 20, 2016	Cornerstone Credit Union League Annual Meeting and Expo held in Oklahoma City I was inducted into their Hall of Fame.

Note: I have left out many that I didn't document. Many times were at the Oklahoma City Nationa Memorial First Person speeches and many times to tour friends and relatives through the Memor

Many of my speeches are a rendition of my story, so I did not feel the need to include those transcripts. However, my acceptance speech for the Cornerstone Credit Union League Hall of Fame Induction Ceremony covered some new ground and was so monumental for me that I wanted to include it.

TRANSCRIPT: Cornerstone Credit Union League Hall of Fame Award Acceptance Speech, April 2016

Wow, this is like the Academy Awards or the Oscars.

......did I really do all of those things or do you have me confused with someone else?

Seriously, There's not enough words in my limited vocularaby to properly express how honored and Grateful I am for this distinguished tribute you have given me tonight.

I would like to take a moment to mention and thank just a few people who have been on this journey with me through the credit union years and since.

First, I particularly want to thank Mike Kloiber who took on the daunting task Of digging up all this data on me, which was quite a chore considering a lot of the destroyed records and not to mention the faded memories that he encountered. You did good Mike.

A Special thanks also to Dick Ensweiler, a true icon in the Credit Union industry , whom I suspect had a role in this scheme. I understand that Dick will be retiring soon after his 52 years . 52 years???? I'm thinking that I may give Him my contact information because he is probably going to need some good advise from time to time on just how to "let it all go" and just stop smell the roses.

I also want to thank a special friend
Mark Kelly who has kept me abreast of a lot of the credit union news throughout the years since my retirement. I miss Mark when I travel these days because He consistently insisted on carrying my luggage

when we traveled to Credit Union Conferences and meetings representing Oklahoma when we were both League board members as well as all of the KOMA meetings we attended.

I'm sure there are many others in this room tonight that I should Thank also who had a part in my long credit union career. You taught me the ropes in those early years, then believed in me enough to elect me to some of those . committees and positions that I served on, and then you came to my rescue when Tragedy struck the Credit Union. 22 credit unions sent me 58 staff members who played a huge part In the miracle, of the survival of FECU.

A personal thanks to Lynette Leonard and her staff who have been diligent through the years since the OKC tradegy keeping the legacy of FECU alive. Five of my staff members remain there today. The credit union is now called Allegiance as I'm sure you know. Actually, I'm still trying to learn how to spell it , but maybe I"ll get there someday.

In looking over the room tonight, I'm thinking that There are many of you that were probably still in High school during most of my credit union career, and I Just recently crunched the numbers and realized that My buddy Mark Kelly was only 9 years old when I was beginning my very first credit union job. You've made me proud.

So I say to you youngsters, you have chosen a great career path, and I wish you much success.

I was blessed and am so grateful, for these past 21 years I was given that I refer to as " my bonus years" These bonus years has given me some time to give back to my community and my church, allowed me to see my hair turn blonde,
three grandkids grow to become adults, and responsible for my newest title "Great Grandmother.". So far

there are 4 of those ' little greats"as I call them,
three living, and one who has already beat me to Heaven. I just found out a few days ago that another one will be here in September.

I would be remiss if I didn't remember to thank my family for all of their love and support throughout my long credit union journey and still there for me.
. My son Terry RoseAnd his wife Ginna are with me tonight. Incidentally, he is the one responsible for my credit union career. You see, when he was about 8 or 9 years old, it was apparent that he was going to need a mouth full of expensive braces, so I quit being his cub scout den mother and became his working Mother.

I recently was given a copy of the Cornerstone
Credit Union Leagues official magazine, which incidentally
Is quite beautifully done, and read your
Theme for this meeting: Passion, purpose and Profession.
I was quite pleased to also see that the old motto from
Back in my day: "People Helping People" has not been put
on the shelf but is still alive and well. I know firsthand how that works.

In closing, I'd like to express again my heartfelt thanks
for this very special tribute tonight. I've had a few awards down
through the years but at my age, they are few and far between, if ever,
but I gotta tell ya, this one tonight has "toped them all.

*Yes, I see that I misspelled "topped." This is a scanned copy of the actual speech document.

Fortunately, my speech was on my own lectern and not handed out to the guests!

Chapter 4
Trixie: Lessons From My Youth

I am a firm believer that I am the sum total of my life experiences. My life cannot be defined by one single moment or event. In fact, *no one's* life can be *defined* by one single moment or event.

Before you disagree, think about what I said.

I did not say that no one's life can be *"changed"* by an event. I said it can't be *"defined."* Sure, an experience can lead to changes in your thinking or alter the way you proceed with life, but I truly do not believe that a person's entire life can be reduced to one moment.

For example, I certainly became a more grateful person after having survived the Oklahoma City Bombing.

However, at my core, I am Florence Rogers not "because" of the bombing.

I am Florence Rogers because of the heartbreaks, triumphs, ups, downs, disappointments, confusion, mentors, mentees, parents, how I grew up, how I raised my sons, and lessons that I learned about myself and about others through my journey.

Mother Goose

Even the title of this book is influenced by a childhood discovery of my love of geese. As I author this decades after the bombing, I wistfully think back to my childhood living in the country 8 miles away from town.

A couple of nights each year during early fall, just a little after dark, my father would come and wake up my siblings and I: "Get up kids. The geese are going over!" It was the most beautiful sight I had ever laid eyes on. Lit only by the moonlight, we would observe hundreds of geese gathered at a time to take flight in unison."

I didn't realize it at the time, but that illustrative vision of nature planted seeds of leadership patterns that I often modeled after the flight patterns and habits of geese.

I always knew that college was not financially an option for me, but that visual lesson gave me a quite an education.

Indeed, life itself is a better teacher than any classroom, and as I author this at 80+ years old, I have made lots of notes along the way. Much of what I have learned has come full circle right back to that little house in Minco, Oklahoma where I was raised.

My humble beginnings are such a part of me that I want to share them with you. Hope you enjoy these stories from my childhood as much as I enjoy telling them!

My Parents, The Innovators

Psychologists and behavioral counselors long debated whether a person's *environment* or their *genetics* play the most influential role in their development. Most of them have now concluded that both aspects hold equal or nearly equal levels of influence.

My life is a textbook example of that indeed "both" is the answer.

At various times in my life, I've had to innovate by making do with what was in front of me and then creating something new from that.

Whether it was *leading* the rebuild of the Federal Employees Credit Union after the bombing or *surviving* on a beginner's salary as a young professional woman in the 1950s or 60s or *stretching* one end to meet the other during a brief time that I was a single mother, I knew how to survive and create.

Mother Goose

During most stages of my life, I've had to work hard. Very few things have come easily to me. I have had to roll up my sleeves, dig in, go after what I want, and outlast the opposition.

I garnered many of the traits necessary for that type of endurance from both parents. Those traits are "in my blood" from their genes, and they're in my psyche from the lessons I learned by watching them.

My parents were Lee and Lucy Hacker married in 1930. Five years later, I was born.

My dad, Lee, was born on January 12, 1897 in Williamson County, Texas and was a veteran of World War I. After 30 days at sea, his unit landed in France on Nov 11, 1918, the same day that the Armistice was signed to end the fighting on land, seas, and air.

Can you believe that? At 21, my father had already traveled overseas, began to fight in one of the largest conflicts in world history, and seen it end!

After about a month, his unit was returned to the United States via the New York Harbor.

Dad often spoke about the impressive Statue of Liberty he saw upon his return and how moving it was to see America again. He was so glad to be home!

After his return, Dad married his first wife, Pearl Brents, and they lived close to Stratford, Oklahoma in a small community called Six Shooter.

They had one son, William Lee, born November 30, 1920. Shortly after William's birth, Dad and Pearl divorced and Dad settled in the Minco, Oklahoma area where he met my mother, the lovely Lucy Mitchum.

Mom was 12 years Dad's junior and they were married on the 15th of March 1930. She was 20, and he was 32.

Lucy and two of her sisters, Rose and Ivy, married Lee and two of his brothers, Ben and Irven. Those 3 families produced 18 children that I always referred to as "the double cousins".

My dad didn't have a formal education, but he understood enough about economics to provide for our family through creative ways. We didn't have much, but we seemed to have all that we needed.

Dad leased the land where I was born from one of the indigenous people who had lived there for many years. The lease was negotiated with the Native American owner and was to be paid annually after harvest.

I still remember the eerie feeling of playing in the yard or doing chores, and then suddenly a man's frame from the darkness of the woods would appear among the trees. Never did this man just show up in the yard or at the house. He would remain at the edge of the woods until my Dad was notified by one of us children running around or by my mother—who had the sharpest eyes on the farm—that they had a visitor.

Dad would always have the lease money ready. Sometimes, it was hidden throughout the house or in other areas on the grounds, but it was always there.

Dad would walk to the edge of the woods, exchange the money for our lease, have a smoke without words, and the man would simply disappear into the woods until the next year.

My family named that place the "Indian Lease" for obvious reasons, and we often refer to it as such to this day.

After a few years on the "Indian lease", Mom and Dad found and purchased an 80-acre farm. The land was a beautiful sight because it had several acres of grape vineyards, and another several acres of mature, neatly trimmed blackberry bushes.

The grapes and the blackberries were there for a reason. The prohibition of alcohol was still in effect during the early 1930s, and the Dutch immigrant who sold the farm to my parents had been known to make a little wine on the side and stored it in his basement root cellar. I recall customers who came to the farm for wine only to be disappointed that the Dutch man was gone.

The fruitful land had also come with a modest two-bedroom house with a large kitchen. Our water came from an underground cistern of purified rain-water, and there was an outhouse about 30 yards away and conveniently down-wind!

My parents decided to use the open-room basement root cellar for storing canned goods instead of wine production. What a great find for my parents to continue raising their new family! They "officially" put their stamp on the land as being "owned by Mr. and Mrs. Lee and Lucy Hacker."

My Siblings

Earlier, I mentioned that my dad, Lee, had fathered a son, William Lee, during his first marriage.

We reunited with my half brother when he was around 17 or 18. He sought out my dad and showed up at our house one day, and he became close with all of us.

We called him "Bill". Bill served in the US Coast Guard in the Pacific Theatre during WW II. He was a chef aboard a Navy ship during his military assignment.

When the war ended, Bill settled in Booker, TX where he married and raised two daughters. Bill died in December, 2003 at the age of 83.

Six years into the start of The Great Depression and four years prior to World War II, I was born on June 3, 1935 on my parents' farm in Minco, OK.

I was the third of the four Hacker children.

My brothers, Bobby, and Donald were the first and second born, and my sister, Joellyn, is the baby, born four years after me.

I was quite a small baby—so much so that it caused my father to exclaim: "What a little trick she is!" Subsequently, I was bestowed with my childhood nickname "Trixie."

Even as I write this in my 80s, whenever I reconnect with a friend or relative who knew me back then, it is not uncommon that they call me "Trixie" instead of Florence.

When my brothers were of age, they were drafted to fight in the Korean War. Mom wrote one of our senators and requested that they be transferred to the same unit.

The military usually did not grant such requests, as it could put the potential for loss of family members at a greater risk. Her request was compelling and was honored.

Bobby possessed true "oldest child" traits.

He was a good soldier and rose to rank of sergeant. Don was a corporal, but he was a tough soldier and served on the front lines where he served as an artillery-man.

Don's ears were terribly damaged from the large caliber firearms, and his hearing was badly impaired for the rest of his life.

Staying true to his resilient and adventurous nature, he worked for the electric company after his military service on a job that required him to climb the wooden power poles.

They didn't have the modern gear used today, so this was a physically taxing job. Don completely wore out his ankles wearing the boots with sharp metal spikes that were used for climbing the poles. Don suffered a broken hip when he was 83, and although it caused a decline in his health, that tough guy stuck around for five more years!

As rugged as Don was, he was equal parts charming with a sweet personality. Even in a compromised physical condition, he was "a bright star" at the Veterans Center in Norman, Oklahoma, and the nurses would fight over who would tend to him.

I was the "different" one of the children. I liked to play but not all of the time. I loved to read, and my brothers would complain to my mother because I would go to the next room by myself and get lost in a book. They felt I should be in the living room with the rest of the family entertaining them. They'd whine: "Mom, make her come in here where we can see her." Mom wouldn't bother me, though. She told them to keep playing and leave me be.

We had no electricity on the farm, but we had carbide lights powered with water and acetylene. People thought we were kind of "fancy" for that.

When Dad went to bed, he required the entire house to be dark, but I loved reading so much that I'd sneak a flashlight to bed and turn it on under my covers. My love of reading endures to this day, and I often find myself taken away to magical places, all in the quiet of my home.

Yip! Yip! School, Cows, and Horses

I spent the first five years of school in Oak Hill, a little one room school house.

When my sister, Joellyn, and I were really young, our brothers walked us to school, but once I turned 11 years old, my sister and I rode a horse to school.

The horse was named Lady, and she was a family friend. We securely tied Lady to a wooden post before heading inside to class, but her free spirit would occasionally overcome her, and she would break loose!

Word would get to my dad that our horse got loose, and then it would be a whole process to get her back to our farm.

Mother Goose

Growing up on a farm taught me time management and created an awareness of responsibilities and task managing. (Later in my life I learned it was called multi-tasking.)

After school, I was instructed to get home in a timely manner and run the cows' home. We had about 7 or 8 of them. I'd holler or make some type of "Yip! Yip!" noise and herd them into the barn.

The cows were a main source of our livelihood and survival. Mom sold cream, so our cows were milked every day and the cream was separated from the actual milk and bottled in cream sized bottles.

Dad would slaughter a calf in the fall in order to feed us through the winter. The local grocer would butcher and wrap the beef for us in white butcher paper, mark each piece as to what it contained, and store in a locked freezer.

We had a key to access it as we needed it. My brothers worked in the fields. We had our own little ecosystem, and we were self-sustained!

When Oak Hill closed, I finally experienced what it was like to ride a bus to town and attended school there.

My school days were peppered with historical events. Growing up in the mid-1930s, 1940s, and early 1950s was an interesting time!

I was hungry for knowledge, and was always known to be a good student who never caused any problems in class. I remember that the sugar and gas rations after World War II got me into trouble at school.

Kids send texts now, but back then, we used pencils and paper. My cousin, Ann, who was not one of my double cousins, wrote me a note in class asking when my family was going to visit relatives for our family vacation. I wrote her back: “We can’t go! Remember, gas is rationed,” and the teacher reprimanded us for passing notes during class. Ann was so beautiful. She was one of my favorite cousins, and we remained close until she died from cancer in 2018.

Seventeen Going On Eighteen

My parents had a good marriage. Not only did they love each other and raise 4 kids in that union, but they also worked in tandem with each other on the farm and in family decision-making. It seemed that they were always in harmony, and I wanted that same happiness for my life.

I knew that I wanted to make my own money and have a professional life outside of what women were normally expected to do in those days, but I also knew that I wanted someone to love me the way my dad loved my mom, and I wanted to love someone the way that my mom loved my dad.

That's why the one thing I remember them getting crossed at each other about is so funny.

Whenever we prepared to travel somewhere as a family, Dad would rush us all into the car insisting that us kids needed to be sitting in the backseat with mom in the passenger's seat ready to go when he was ready to go.

Then, right before we drove off, Dad would stop and check the oil. This would drive my mom absolutely crazy! Why did he stress that we all get into the car, and he hadn't already checked the oil?

Mom would sit there irritated as my dad tinkered under the hood.

When I think of this now, I find it pretty funny and it still brings a chuckle.

Other than my dad's oddly timed car oil checks, my parents were happy, and I wanted that in my adult life.

Back then, once a young person hit 17, we knew that 18 was around the corner, and that was the "marrying and moving out on your own" age!

During my senior year in high school, I was introduced to and fell in love with a young man named Kenneth.

He had a unique and magnetic way of drawing people to him. Kenneth wasn't unattractive, but he wasn't the most handsome guy either. He just oozed a charisma and confidence, and it seemed like everyone liked him for it. It drew me to him.

Our generation had a real sense of wanting to be "a part of something" and contribute to society. Kenneth went off to the Korean War just like my brothers and so many other young men had, but I vowed to wait for him.

Kenneth's family and I had developed a great relationship, and they moved me into a small home in Oklahoma City, where I lived right after high school. There, I was to prepare it for Kenneth to return to after the war.

Thank goodness my mother didn't discourage my love for reading when my brothers complained about it. That love coupled with my overall thirst for knowledge worked out well for me. In 1953, I graduated from Minco High School as the valedictorian.

Shortly afterward, Kenneth's sister, Bettie, helped me find a job working for the Southwestern Bell Telephone Company in Oklahoma City. She drove me to the interview, and I was able to use her family's phone for the callback notifying me that I had been hired. I was off to work in the big city!

Bettie and I grew to become good friends. I even babysat her son, Richard. He was the cutest kid. I learned that Richard had committed suicide at a very young age, and it burns in my mind as one of my earliest brushes with sudden tragedy.

One day, Bettie came into the house that her family had helped me move into and informed me that I had to move out. Kenneth had come home from his time in the Navy, docked in Los Angeles, and married the first person he saw off the boat.

Here, I had been setting up house while he was gone, and now, I was having to move and start on a new life adventure alone.

At Southwestern Bell, I met my co-worker, Sue. She and I rented an apartment together, and we led busy lives as working girls.

I was very fortunate to have been hired by Southwestern Bell, and that was quite an accomplishment in those days. I worked as a long distance operator and usually pulled a 1:00 to 10:00pm shift.

There wasn't much time for a social life, but it was good money, and I was grateful for it.

As life would have it, Sue turned out to be more than a roommate but as someone who would change my life forever. She introduced me to Dean Rose with whom I ended up marrying and raising two sons.

The tapestry of life is quite amazing isn't it? Sue and I met for a reason. I believe we meet *all* people for a reason. One path intertwines with the other and leads us in our destiny steps.

Here are my diary excerpts which display the musings of a young woman in a hurry. I couldn't wait to get out and make my mark in the world.

May 12, 1953 Tuesday. Went to school. I graduated this night. Won the American Legion Award. Shorthand award, Valedictory and Honor Society.

May 17th Leaving for Senior trip which consisted of a trip to Grand Lake, Bartlesville, Woolaroc Museum, Ponca City where we saw the Pioneer Woman statue, and have photos of myself swinging from her arm.

May 28, Thursday. I had planned to go to the city to find a job, but I decided to wait until Monday.

June 2nd Had two interviews and shopped a little.

June 3rd Wednesday. Ironed for my friend Bettye. Today I am 18 years old. Gee I feel old.

June 11th Bettye took me to the telephone office. I filled out an application form. Sure hope I get on.

June 29th Started to work. Had dinner on the company. Nice. I'm gonna love it.

August 20 through August 31st .Telephone Company on strike. I returned to work on the 31st of Aug.

FAST FORWARD TO SEPTEMBER, 1953

Sept. 22nd Tuesday. I was off today, so I went to hospital to visit a lady from my hometown, then I met my roommate. Her and I shared a little garage apartment on the north side of Oklahoma City. We met at Katz Drugstore.

She spotted a handsome soldier that she apparently knew and asked him to join us at our table since the place was crowded. Before long, she had to go to work and left me there with this guy. (It turned out that he was her x brother-in-law).
He ordered a ham sandwich and didn't eat it. I found out his name was Merlin Dean Rose and that he had just returned to the states from having served in Korea. He took me riding in his newly purchased 50 Mercury. We went to a drive in theatre where "Cruzing Down the River" was playing.

Sept 27th Dean left for Kansas City to visit a brother and wife who had just had twins.
Nothing on the pages until I pick up again on

Oct. 24th. Dean drove back from camp Chaffee to see me. I was sure tickled to see him.

Oct. 25th. He left early to go back to camp. He will be assigned to Camp Polk, LA. We plan to marry Dec. 23rd.

Dec. 7, 1954 I got my engagement ring. It's beautiful. I can hardly wait until I'm Mrs. Rose.

Dec. 23rd. Got to Sallisaw about 10:30 and went to see Baker Wall the judge. He began right away to try to marry us. We had a medical examination and had quite a time going through all the rules. At 12;00 noon, we became man and wife.

Dec. 25th. My brand new husband and I spent Christmas with my folks in Minco between my telephone company working hours.

Till We Meet Again, Mom and Dad

It doesn't matter how old we live to be, we never really "get over" our parents dying. We don't "get past it" either. Rather, we just adjust to life without them as best we can.

Dad died from lung cancer in September 1961 at the young age of 64.

For extra money between crops, he worked a seasonal job harvesting cotton at a cotton gin in town.

His job was to get up on a big platform like a deck so he could put the big suction machine-line together, and while the suction was happening, the cotton lint would get into his lungs as he inhaled.

Over the years, the lint accumulated. Couple that with smoking, and it's not a healthy environment for the respiratory system.

The doctors at the V.A. Medical center commented about the cotton fibers they had found in his lungs, and thought that it was like a secondary filter for the tobacco.

It also was like a sponge, soaking up the tar and holding it there.

My mother lived many years after our dad died. A few years after losing Dad, oil was discovered on her land which opened up a new world for her.

She had struggled to hold on to the land, and had taken jobs in town cleaning houses, and even drove to Aero Commander at Wiley Post Air Port daily, to polish air plane parts.

Her first check came in the mail from the oil company, and it was $13,000. The next month the check came again and it was $10,000. Oh man, she was set and could live a much more secure life as she aged!

She eventually developed and succumbed to Alzheimer's in 1988. It was so strange seeing a woman whose eyes were so sharp and mind was so quick suffer from a degenerative brain disease, so when she finally moved to Heaven, I was relieved for her.

As I write this, my sister, Joellyn, and I are the remaining two Hacker siblings.

Our oldest brother, Bobby, joined our Mom and Dad in December of 2013.

Don joined them in May of 2020 on Mother's Day. I miss them both, but losing Don hit me particularly hard. For years, Don and I lived less than half an hour away from each other, and we had enjoyed several laughs and great visits at the Veterans Center where he resided until his death.

As woman in her mid-80s, I spend a lot of time reflecting, and these memories increase in value as each precious moment passes.

So much of "who I am" including any professional achievements and my life as a mother, grandmother, and great-grandmother, I owe to Lee and Lucy Hacker. They set in place an example to live by, and their children saw that example every day.

Till we all meet again, Mom and Dad. You two, Bobby, and Don leave a "Heavenly carbide light" on for us!

Chapter 5
Womanhood

So much of this book is about the bombing and my professional life, but I want to dedicate this chapter as a window into my personal life.

Women are often not viewed multi-dimensionally.

We are erroneously perceived as "career women who only care about professional advancement" or "homemakers whose minds are absorbed with dinners, soccer practices, and kids."

However, I—*like most other women*—am "all woman." As ambitious as I was professionally, I was equally desirable for a solid home life.

Financial management is what I *did*—not who I *am.* I longed to love and to be loved.

Like any human, I didn't always govern my personal life with my head. My heart often took over...and you know what? That's okay. It means I'm human.

Dean Rose

Ages 17 and 18 were whirlwinds for me!

As I mentioned in chapter 4, I grew up in an era where once a young person hit 17, we knew that 18 was around the corner, and that was the "marrying and moving out on your own" age.

How differently we do things today! College and professional careers have taken precedent over marrying and reproducing.

Kids may live with their parents throughout college. Some may move out and then move back in after struggling to find a job that pays enough for them to live in this much more expensive and much more complicated world—especially after having been saddled with student loans.

Not so in the 1950s! I left the house, got a job, and was setting up for marriage—the first of which was to Dean Rose who was introduced to me by my co-worker, Sue.

I look back on 1953 in amazement. In one year, I had landed a "big job" at the Southwestern Bell Telephone Company, courted and married Dean Rose, and moved to Louisiana where Dean was stationed in the Army.

Dean and I were married for 20 years. It's amazing how different we were at the beginning of our marriage than at the end of our marriage. I, for one, was 18 when we married and 38 when we divorced. A whole lot of changing happens during those ages!

I was a teenager when I married Dean. My frontal lobe wasn't even fully developed yet! The Health Encyclopedia of the University of Rochester puts it best:

> *It doesn't matter how smart teens are or how well they scored on the SAT or ACT. Good judgment isn't something they can excel in, at least not yet.*
>
> *The rational part of a teen's brain isn't fully developed and won't be until age 25 or so.*
>
> *In fact, recent research has found that adult and teen brains work differently. Adults think with the prefrontal cortex, the brain's rational part. This is the part of the brain that responds to situations with good judgment and an awareness of long-term consequences. Teens process information with the XXXmygdale. This is the emotional part.*
>
> *In teen's brains, the connections between the emotional part of the brain and the decision-making center are still developing—and not always at the same rate. That's why when teens have overwhelming emotional input, they can't explain later what they were thinking. They weren't thinking as much as they were feeling.*

Don't take all of this scientific information the wrong way. I do not regret marrying Dean Rose.

He gave me two beautiful boys whom I call "the roses" to this day—a perfect double entendre nickname for those two loves of my life.

He was a wonderful father to my sons and an overall good person...

HOWEVER, if I were to tell you that emotions weren't the driving force behind my decision to marry Dean, I would be robbing you of the full context of that relationship.

I was a teenage girl who had just been jilted by Kenneth whom I had been setting up shop for while he was off to war, and, according to 1950s standards, my clock was ticking!

I had an affinity for handsome men in uniform because I was drawn to men who showed ambition, purpose, and the charisma to accomplish things.

A uniform—especially a military uniform—seemed to shout those attributes to me.

I was also the type of girl who liked "different," and Dean checked all of those boxes, so when I fell for him, I fell hard and fast which is why we were married less than a year after meeting and courting.

So many things about Dean intrigued me.

I was attracted to him when I first saw him at the Katz drugstore in downtown Oklahoma City.

He wasn't very tall for a man—around 5'7"—but he had a nice build and filled out his military uniform nicely. He had tan hair, blue eyes, and a gorgeous smile.

I love a good story, and Dean had several. He had a big personality, and, in animated fashion, he would tell stories about his twin sister and him.

My family really liked Dean, and, for women, this is particularly important. Generally, after men marry, they "cleave to their wife's family" (Genesis 2:24, Ephesians 5:31) while women tend to draw closer to their own families—especially when their mothers jump in to help with the babies, etc.

It's interesting that people think this is a secular concept, but it's actually clearly stated in the Bible. Therefore, when my family took to Dean, it was a plus for me.

He would always tell them funny stories and make everybody in the room smile—even my protective father and brothers!

Dean's stories about his sister were cute, but, as I mentioned earlier, I like "different," so it was his adventurous stories that I enjoyed the most.

I like people and things that are unique, out of the box, and top notch (just like my business suits and that blue Lincoln I loved so much)!

Dean fascinated me with his stories of leaving home at a very young age to join the Ringling Brothers circus. He traveled all over the country with them!

This was huge in my eyes because I had not been to many places outside of Oklahoma, and, even when I did go, it was on family trips to see relatives. It certainly was not for circus showbiz!

When Dean was barely old enough, he joined the Army, served in the Korean War, and achieved the rank of Sergeant First Class (SFC) during his nine year enlistment.

Dean was six years older than me. When you add his charisma, life experiences, and good looks, Dean's version of age 24 just seemed so much older and mature in my 18 year old emotionally driven eyes, so I fell for him hard and fast! We married in 1953 after only months of courting!

Not long after the Army had stationed us in Louisiana, we were moved to Kansas and then to Colorado where our two sons, Jerry and Terry were born.

Dean was such a good soldier and was even placed in charge of training other soldiers. After he left the Army in 1956, we settled our newly expanded family in Oklahoma City.

Dean could always sell himself quite well when seeking job opportunities.

Once he landed the job, he could do just about anything that he was required to do. He secured several different jobs with various positions, but he never made a lot of money.

I sold Avon for awhile and was a den mother for the Cub Scouts where Jerry and Terry were active along with Dean who was a Scoutmaster, but it wasn't long before our ever-piling bills led me to seek work outside of the home, and that's when my career in the credit union started in 1965.

Having found my calling in the financial industry, I flourished pretty quickly, after only six years on that career track, I was hired by the Federal Employees Credit Union as its CEO in 1971. Only two years later in 1973, Dean and I divorced.

The demise of our marriage was somewhat of a slow boil that started when Dean left the military.

While I managed to find a professional passion, Dean bounced from job to job. He would quit a job at a moment's notice and go hunt for more.

Looking back on it, I feel that his struggle to stick with an occupation was rooted in the fact that his true passion was the Army.

Therefore, anything that wasn't military-based didn't seem to interest him—or at least it didn't seem to light his fire.

Dean was a man who found his identity and purpose in his work, and he felt that my role as his wife was to be solely focused on rearing our kids and keeping up our home.

Well, I was too smart to be relegated to only those things. I am naturally, a gifted multi-tasker, so being a wife and mother were only a part of what I felt called to do with my life. I didn't find my entire identity in biological roles. On top of which, being the organized "nuts and bolts" type of person that I am, there was no way that I was going to stay home and watch our finances continue to strain when I was an able-bodied, intelligent woman fully capable of holding a job myself.

Not only was I smart, but I was also curious. I always have been.

I enjoy reading and escaping to "other worlds." I watch and read the news to keep up with what's going on in the world, and as a young wife and mother, I was simultaneously an ambitious young woman. I wanted the best that the world had to offer for Dean, our sons, and me.

Dean loved Jerry and Terry. Make no mistake about that. He even became a scoutmaster, and I was a den mother for the boys' cub scouts troop. However, I felt, there was always "another layer" of life under which new jewels could be discovered.

I was a future-minded person, so I wanted our sons to see and achieve things that Dean and I might have never dreamed of.

I knew that if that was going to happen, that Dean and I would need to reach for the stars ourselves and show our boys by example that new levels could be attained.

Dean was different. Perhaps, having married him at the tender age of 18, I was too mesmerized by his adventurous Ringling Bros. stories and movie star good looks to realize this.

He was content to get by on making the ends meet by the skin of our teeth each month, and that surprised me. His ambitions seemed to leave him, and in my opinion, he stopped growing.

Even when Dean and I got to the point where I knew we could afford better things, Dean didn't want to spend the money.

Things were "good enough," he said.

Don't get me wrong. I was grateful for the little house we lived in. It was built in 1953, and we moved into it in 1957. It was cute, but it was small, and with two growing boys, I wanted to expand.

Not only that, I was raised in a very modest home, and I had "every girl's dream" of having a big house with a big yard. It didn't have to be a mansion, but I wanted more—or at least the hope that we were going to get more.

Dean's complacency took the wind out of my little sails, and I felt that I couldn't hold on to any of my dreams with the hopes of any of them actually coming true. It was actually quite depressing.

When I returned to the workforce, our youngest son, Terry, was eight years old, and our oldest son, Jerry, was nine and ½. They are 18 months apart.

By the time Dean and I divorced, Jerry had already married and left home, and Terry was a junior in high school.

As you can see from the way I dreamed and the way Dean stayed on autopilot, our marriage was a ticking time bomb, but I truly feel that it was my credit union rise that ultimately drove us apart.

Dean was very envious of my successes. He wanted me at home with the boys 24/7, so when I wasn't at work, he would send my youngest son, Terry, with me on errands. Dean really thought that Terry could be the lookout in case I cheated on him or something!

I would frequently have to attend evening meetings. Dean knew there would be men there, and it drove him absolutely crazy.

This is why I respectfully don't advise any ambitious person to marry a person who doesn't also have goals, dreams, and passions outside of you to keep themselves occupied.

The more I was absent, the more, he sat in the house and stewed about what it was that I could possibly be doing.

The financial industry is a predominately male-driven field, but it was even more so in the late 60s and early 70s.

In order to get ahead, I had to be seen.

I had to be seen at meetings. I had to be seen at volunteer opportunities. I had to be seen with peers at other credit unions to remain "a part of them" and "in the know."

What's discussed in those atmospheres is what gives a person the insight needed to know how to move in those circles.

Not only was I a woman in a man's role, but the actual nature of those roles are very political, calculating, and competitive.

I had a double layer of obstacles to overcome at every turn, and I had to be twice as good in order to show my worth. I knew I was privileged to have those roles—especially when I was finally hired on as the Federal Employees Credit Union CEO—so I wanted to operate at the highest version of myself.

The only males Dean wanted me to talk about were him and our boys, but my colleagues were males, so the: "How was work today?" conversations were not very pleasant.

As with any type of bitterness, Dean's festered because he nursed it instead of extinguishing it. He would constantly ask: "Where've you been?" when I had already explained ahead of time that I had a meeting. When possible, I would even give him a heads up days ahead of time, and that still was not good enough for him.

Terry, being the more curious of my two sons, would often hear these harsh conversations. He would lay in the floor next to the furnace in his bedroom. There was an air pocket at the bottom where the natural gas burners were, and he could hear Dean and me through it.

Dean and I would be getting ready for bed, and that's when Dean decided to close the door and commence our big argument.

I would hold my own and yell right back at him, but I absolutely hated it. I have never thrived in contention, so this was absolutely miserable for me, and, because I was flustered, I am not very sure that I communicated my side of the argument well to Dean.

He probably still would not have listened anyway, but, in essence, what I as trying to say was: "I have to go be seen. I have to go and do this in order to continue to progress and compete with the big boys."

Little Terry hated to hear how harshly Dean spoke to me. It was verbal abuse, and Terry just did not understand the reason for it. He thought his dad was being completely insufferable, and he became very protective of me. To this day, Terry lives only a few miles from me, and he constantly checks on me.

Jerry and my grandchildren do as well, but there is an "extra layer of protective covering" from Terry. It is amazing how childhood events affect our adulthood outlooks on life.

As I write this book, Terry is in his mid-60s, but that aspect of our relationship has never changed.

Instead of internalizing and mimicking this aspect of his father's behavior, Terry instead learned that this was not how a man should speak to a woman, and he knew at an early age that he just could not give this much energy into rage-filled arguments with a spouse.

My oldest son, Jerry, absolutely hated conflict.

He didn't want to fight, and he didn't want to hear fighting, so his method was to withdraw.

He didn't talk about it with Terry and instead opted to stay in his own world.

As soon as Jerry was old enough, he moved out of the house and got married.

While Dean was otherwise a very good father to the boys, he failed in this area, and I feel that Jerry's swift exit of our home was a method of escape for him.

It pained me to move on, but I felt I had no other choice but to divorce Dean. His jealousy broke our covenant.

However, with time, age, and experiences, I've grown a more complete perspective on the matter detached from youthful emotions, and I conclude with this: my young adult years contained beautiful memories with Dean, and those are the ones I choose to reflect on.

Dean has since joined my parents and brothers. He was the father of my beautiful sons, and, through them, I have life's most precious gifts in grandchildren and great-grandchildren. For that, I will always be grateful.

Don Rogers

Two years after divorcing Dean and four years after being named CEO of the Federal Employees Credit Union, I married Donald R. Rogers on April 25, 1975.

We divorced in 1990, but Don was still working in the federal building at the time of the bombing in 1995.

Don and I had actually already met prior to our romantic involvement.

When I first began my stint at the credit union, it was housed in the US courthouse building, and Don worked as an electrician for the General Services Administration (GSA) whose building was nearby.

This is how the GSA employees who rescued me were able to recognize me on the day of the bombing. I had already known several of them through my marriage to Don and from working in a nearby office.

Eventually, Don landed on our credit committee where he served for several years, so I saw him very often.

He had advanced from the maintenance department to becoming the building manager for the entire Alfred P. Murrah Federal Building where he was serving at the time of the bombing and sustained injuries.

Don was very handsome, and he was also a member of the Oklahoma Air National Guard, so you know me...That pushed my “affinity-for-handsome-men-in-uniforms” button!

Don stood about 6’2” or 3” and was very well built with beautiful dark brown eyes and thick, very black hair. Even in his old age as I write this, he still has a full head of beautiful gray hair. Paired with my tailored suits, never ending lipstick, and perfectly coiffed red hair, we were a sight! We were frequently complimented as a great-looking couple.

Don might have been what many women would call “the perfect husband.” Of course, no one is actually perfect, but he sure was close.

We had a very enjoyable 15-year marriage in large part because Don was just so easy-going.

My career was never an issue with him. In fact, we traveled a lot, and he would attend some of my credit union meetings across the globe. He was a fun travel partner and a hot date to those conferences!

As it is with many second marriages, Don I were both more mature and had a stronger handle on who we were as individuals, so we did not engage in immature, emotionally-driven arguments.

Don was his own man, and I was my own woman, so we didn't have the added challenge of growing up and becoming adults *on top of* trying to rear a family like Dean and I did because we had both already advanced past that stage and had our own adult children.

As great as the union between Don and I was, our independence might have actually been the element that created distance between us.

Our greatest strength ended up being a weakness. I made more money than Don, and that wasn't a problem for him, but we kept separate bank accounts, and, at times, that contributed to a feeling of us living separate lives.

We were both busy, and I was only becoming busier, so, as much as Don was with me, he was away from me, too. I might leave the house and say: "I'm headed off to (wherever it was that I was going)," and he would do the same. Before we knew it, there might be consecutive weeks where we were like ships passing each other in the night.

In retrospect, perhaps Don was so careful not to repeat what I had told him I disliked from my marriage to Dean that he pulled back a little too much. Instead of me effectively communicating that I wanted more closeness, I just let it roll on, and before I knew it, my beautiful marriage had ended.

Don and I remain friends, and I have even maintained close relationships with his family members.

Many of his nieces and nephews still call me Aunt Florence! Don and I were married when my first grandson, Chad, was born and those two have kept their bond throughout all these years.

I still see them together quite often, and, at 40+ years old, Chad still calls him Papa Don!

Kenneth Returns

As I wrote at the beginning of this chapter, I'm human which means I'm multi-dimensional. As deliberate as I was with my professional life, at times, in my personal life, I could be exactly the opposite. I found myself in positions where I lead with my heart while completely abandoning my head, and my relationship with Kenneth is a textbook example of that.

Do you remember Kenneth? The guy whom I'd planned to set up home for while he was serving in the Korean War, but then he deflated my hopes when he married another girl? The guy I had known when I was a teenager?

Well, for a time after my second divorce, I was in a relationship with him. That relationship went so left that I still sometimes look back and wonder: "Why did I even give that the time of day?"

Then, I remember my soft heart. I remember my girlish curiosity of "What if-ism" and thinking that maybe—just maybe—my 3rd attempt at love would be the charm as I sought to recapture some of the excitement of my youth.

I wasn't in a mid-life crisis. I have just always loved love—romantic love to be precise.

I was in my 60s and still felt like I had plenty more years to give and receive love in a beautiful relationship.

I heard through some friends that Kenneth had newly become single, so I went for it!

Let's just say that there is a reason some people are in your past, and the majority of them should remain there.

I had romanticized who Kenneth might be.

It was like the guy you crushed on all during high school, and you finally got your chance to be with him—except I was in my 60s! I still got my chance after all those years!

I thought and re-thought...wrote and rewrote...typed and erased trying to determine how much to say and whether or not to even include this part of my life at all, but I ultimately decided to include it so that the readers can "hear" this from someone with life experience: don't put a comma where God has put a period. Many a pastor has cited that, and they're correct.

What I thought was Kenneth's charming personality ended up being manipulative. What I thought was his adventurous spirit ended up being irresponsible. What I thought was his strength ended up being a bad temper.

What I thought was his financial stability ended up draining a large percentage of my hard earned personal revenue. What I thought was handsome converted into: "If I never see that guy again, I'll be just fine."

The bottom line is, for anyone looking to find love later in life, make sure if you reconnect with an old flame that you don't forget why you separated in the first place because it will not end well if that person has not undergone a wholesale character change.

Your front windshield is larger than your rearview mirror. Keep moving forward. God has great things in your future, and you need not let your needy heart impair your judgment and obstruct the path to your destiny.

I don't wallow in regrets because I believe that we learn from both the positive and the negative experiences and choices of our lives.

Therefore, while regret can be helpful in preventing a repeat of a mistake, regret in and of itself is somewhat of a wasted emotion. However, if I could substitute one set of life choices with better decisions, it would be the set I made with Kenneth allowing it to disrupt my personal peace and rob me of precious time.

Blessed To Pass Down The Blessing

I've been blessed to enjoy every aspect of womanhood, my favorite of which has to be becoming a grandmother.

I have three grandchildren and five great-grandchildren.

In these golden years, I've become more reflective on the important things in life, chief among which are lasting, meaningful relationships. I value the innocence in a child's eyes so much more as a grandparent than I did as a parent.

While I am grateful for technological advances, I sometimes feel that it has robbed the younger generations of their sense of wonder.

In many aspects, technology creates your imagination for you instead of pushing you to use your own. It takes a lot more to "amaze" kids, now.

When I was young, a starry sky with geese crossing over was awe-inspiring.

Now, kids are very digitally oriented. I wish I could bottle up all of the wonder of my childhood and give it to my grandkids.

Christmas in Minco

I have many fond memories of my childhood Christmas seasons in Minco, Oklahoma.

When I was a kid, Santa Claus always showed up at the annual Christmas play at the little country schoolhouse to pass out the sacks of candy, nuts, apples, and oranges. Everyone was so excited to see him.

Usually, one of the local fathers donned the Santa suit. One year, it was my dad. As he went up and down the school aisles greeting the little ones, his red bottoms began to fall off! (Someone had played a trick on him and untied the drawstring when he came in the back door.)

When he got to the seat where my mom, my sister and I were sitting, my mom said: “Santa, you are about to lose your pants,” and she promptly reached out to tie them up.

Everyone at the school participated in the Christmas program and sang all of the traditional Christmas carols. It was a big event for the season and the only social thing that was going on. The farm houses were fairly far apart, so no one did caroling.

Some of the families didn't even have a car. Someone who is accustomed to receiving more "things" at Christmas may view this as "poor people fun," but we were rich in love and tradition.

We were not materialistic. The glee of Santa and the laughter of kids and families brought us such joy. We didn't have fancy toys, but, my goodness, those bags of candy, nuts, and fruit were a true delight to us!

Life was much simpler than it is now. There weren't any televisions, so everyone had to be creative with games and their entertainment. Families were closer.

I don't have memories of any special foods at Christmas although I am sure mom probably killed a big old hen and cooked her. She did raise turkeys every year to sell in the fall, so it is possible we had a turkey now and then for Christmas.

Once I became an adult living in Oklahoma City, I was able to attend church regularly, but, as a child, my family was one of several families who didn't have a church to attend in rural Minco, so I have no memories of church in my early years.

Instead, two missionary ladies from Oklahoma City came to the school once a month to bring the Word of God to the kids. They had a felt board and told us the Bible stories using felt pieces. They gave prizes for the ones of us who memorized the most Bible verses.

I never forgot those little women who brought me my first knowledge of the Bible. They are the reason I knew the Christmas story about the birth of Jesus.

Some of the fathers always cut down a very big cedar tree to bring to the schoolhouse so that we could have a Christmas tree there, and we all made paper decorations and strung popcorn to use for the decorations. We thought it beautiful back in those days. We loved the smell of the fresh cedar tree mixed with the hot apple cider that the mothers brought to the school for the occasion.

We didn't have many Christmas decorations at home. My family always went out in the woods and cut down a cedar tree. They were scratchy and hard to decorate, but that was okay with us.

My family was usually able to go to Chickasha about 20 miles south of Minco to do a little shopping and that was really something to us.

In our minds, Chickasha was a really big city and the Christmas lights and the decorated storefronts were spectacular to the eyes of a child.

I remember those visits to "the big city" quite well. Going up and down the aisles at the dime store and looking at all the neat things was very memorable.

I have no memory of Christmas Eve being anything except another night. Most of our gifts, which were very few, were given to us kids by Santa at the Christmas program at our little school, so by Christmas Day, we had already received our gifts and probably had broken them already.

I don't remember anything special that we did on the actual Christmas Day other than visiting relatives if the weather permitted.

One of the most special Christmas days of my youth occurred on my first ever visit out of the state of Oklahoma. I was a teenager.

One of my brothers was in the Army and stationed in Ft. Bliss, Texas in El Paso. He wasn't going to get to come home as he was preparing to go to Korea. My other brother was at home on leave from the Army, and he would also be headed to Korea soon.

My mom baked all of my brother's favorite cookies and candy and made chicken salad sandwiches and we all loaded in the car and headed for Texas to see him before he had to leave for the War.

He was so glad to get the sandwiches and the homemade cookies. We spent Christmas Day that year walking the streets of Juarez, Mexico which was really exciting and certainly a new experience for my entire family.

I do not recall my mother ever mailing out Christmas cards in the early years of my childhood. First of all, we couldn't afford them, and, secondly, mail was slow and unreliable, so actually, very few families mailed Christmas cards.

However, they did send letters to relatives who lived far away. It cost three cents to mail a letter and six cents for the airmail letters that were sent overseas.

These Christmas memories may seem unimpressive to today's children living in a technology-driven 21st Century, but they were as special to us then as the current Christmases are to the little ones now—and probably more so because nice things were so less common to come by. We found joy in such simple things, and we were much easier to please.

Christmas and Grandkids: Keeping Christmas Classic

As I said previously, I wish I could bottle up all of the wonder of my childhood and give it to my grandkids, and I get as close as I possibly can to that during Christmastime.

I'm a pretty good cook if I may say so myself! I make a mean slow-cooked pot roast, and I very much enjoy baking cookies and pies. I've slowed down on this bit, but when my family comes over, I still manage to whip up a handful of these special dishes whenever my family visits.

I even chopped down a huge cedar one year and had the "grandies" help me decorate it!

Every Christmas, I send out my yearly letter with updates on everything from my community involvement to my little dog, Minni to my church, to scrapbooking, and I often tuck them inside homemade greeting cards. Sending letters is nearly a lost art, and it is always joy-filling to get gleeful responses from my kids and grandkids after having received mine. Of course, you have to wonder if they're happier about the letter or about the cash I've tucked inside of the card!

Check out some of my favorite letters below. In 2019, I used a similar letter and just updated the information with my pen.

December 1996

Dear Family and Friends,

This Christmas season finds me "snuggled" in at home recuperating from surgery on my neck. Had to have a couple of vertebrae "fixed" that were damaged in the fall I took in the Murrah Building. They were able to find a great wrinkle in the front of my neck for the incision so I probably won't even have a scar that shows. My sister spent a week with me making sure I ate and took my pills. We got caught up on all the great old memories, and enjoyed visiting. We made plans for our trip to Australia next February. I have been invited to tell my credit union story to the Australian Credit Unions. We're getting pretty excited about this trip. It's hard not to start packing already.

My travels in 1996 have taken me to Seattle; Toronto; Canada; Pittsburgh, PA; Rochester, N.Y.; Panama City, FL; Park City, Utah; Newport Beach and Anaheim, California. My luggage is showing some wear and tear. Santa needs to bring me some new.

I had a lovely Thanksgiving dinner at Terry and Ginna's. Since I'm not driving yet and having to wear a lovely collar, they had to come get me. This may get a little old, not having much independence. You know how I am.

My trip to Anaheim was in mid November so I put my Christmas decor up before I left. You might say I am ahead of the season. I think I may get a little tired of it all.

My boys and their little families are all fine. Chad is nearly 18. Can you believe it? Jerry's kids are big too. (8 and 10 now) We're planning a big Christmas at my home. Hopefully I'll be able to cook the old favorites. I'm sure I'll be quite tired of frozen pot pies by then.

The credit union is doing great. Have 39 employees now and a branch downtown. Did you see us on 48 Hours last April? My staff is the best! We are quite a little family having come through such a long 18 months together. This will be the longest stretch I've ever been out of the office so we'll see how well things are together I guess. Hopefully, I will be able to go back sometime before Christmas. I have been fairly active in the Memorial Foundation activities and met so many wonderful people this year. I have been instrumental in $17,500 in donations so far for the permanent memorial. Some of the places where I have told our story have given donations to the memorial. Someday there will be a wonderful memorial where so much sorrow occurred.

I hope you and your families have a great holiday season. Don't forget, I'm only 10 minutes from the airport when you are in OKC. I'm really home a lot, even though it might not sound like it and would love to have company. "Girl" dog and I ramble around in this house so there's lots of room. One of my reporter friends stayed with me a couple of times last spring when she was doing our anniversary stories.

Wish this was a funny Christmas letter like the ones I sent in the 60's and 70's, don't you?

Keep in touch and have a Merry Christmas and a Happy New Year.

My warmest regards,

Florence
(Trixie to some of you)

My Christmas letter from 1996

Ancestor Scrapbook Message

Christmas Dec 2008

This Genealogy Scrapbook is dedicated to my three grandchildren:Chad, Amanda and David. It is my hope that it will become a special treasure as you share these memories with my great grandchildren some day, and also serve as a history of their ancestors. I spent many enjoyable hours searching our geaneology and working on this book It was a fun little "labor of love". I traveled many miles down "memory lane",sometimes late into the night.. I learned so much about our family history that I never knew before and I hope you will enjoy some of the stories I have shared with you.. It was impossible to capture all of the good times we all shared over the years, the Christmas Eves, weddings, birthdays, travels, but I hope some of the pictures will spark your own memories.I also hope you will encourage your moms to expand this book to include their family history for you to share with your children, my great granchildren..

My most treasured memories are the Christmas Eves when I gathered my grandchildren around me on the hearth and we took the annual photo while good smells from the kitchen meant that my son's favorite foods were being cooked for them to enjoy. And remember the little pine tree I planted in the back yard to hide the gas meter that you helped decorate many Christmases;. now nearly 30 ft. tall, it's a daily reminder that you too grew up tall and beautiful.

This year I celebrated my 73rd birthday. Someday as you are looking through this book, remember that I was born before television, video games, computers, cell phones, color movies, pizza delivery and a lot of things that you have always had in your lives. I can even remember my excitement as a child when we finally got electricity on the farm where we lived and we never had a telephone until after I graduated and left home.

I have been blessed with wonderful sons, daughter-in=laws and grandchildren. My memories are special treasures, and each one of you holds a special place in my heart. With my love,
MEME

My Christmas letter from 2008

December ~~2018~~ 2019

Dearest Friends and loved ones, Minni absolutely refused to do the annual Christmas letter this year. She told me to skip the cards, and for me to send you a short note recapping our year, but to keep it short with only the highlights. So here's the reader's digest version of ~~2018.~~ 2019.

1. My travels this year took me to Walmart, Walgreens, Doctors offices, PetSmart, Credit Union drive through lane, church on Sundays, and the new Sprouts Grocery store close to my house~~, on opening day~~.
2. Worked several elections~~, including the big one in Nov. Took me several days to get over that one.~~ gave This job up This year!
3. Lost way too many friends and relatives this year, so that meant a whole bunch of funerals. Too many!
4. Florida kids came for Thanksgiving~~, and deer hunting.~~ I got out of cooking a big dinner as the Okc kids had a big spread and the granddaughter also had one.
5. No new great grandkids this year, but all of the current ones are still quite beautiful. Another one due in February! #5
6. ~~Attended a family reunion in hometown Minco in July. That may be the last one, because~~ everyone has gotten so old, and hated the noise from the small children. Didn't have one!
7. I'm writing my memoirs in my spare time, hoping to find someone brave enough to read that stuff someday. Book due soon! Will Ke[ep] you posted so y[ou] can order one!
8. Took a ton of stuff to the credit union free shred day in Sept. so the kids wouldn't hate me if they had to recycle that pile. I now have room to start keeping stuff again. Same Story!
9. They still let me live in my home and haven't taken the car away yet. Same

That's about it for ~~2018~~ 2019. It was an exciting year as you can see, and so glad I could share it with you. !!

Taking time out also to wish each of you a Merry Christmas and a Blessed year in ~~2019~~ 2020. Do keep in touch, life can be short you know!

2019 had few changes!!

Love, Florence (Trixie to a few) and Meme to some. Minni sends her best wishes also. Find me on FaceBook!

My 2018 and 2019 Christmas letter

Grateful Honks From Mother Goose

Grateful HONKS to all of you that stayed on this 2 year migration, honking loudly, and flapping those wings that kept me encouraged to stay on the course until we reached the destination of seeing "MOTHER GOOSE" to the nest.

"Beautiful HONKS" to so many of you that have stayed in the flight pattern to reach this destination.

Very extraordinary HONKS to the goslings that rushed in so quickly to start the rebuilding of a new nest for our credit union: Raymond, Brad, Joe, Bobbi, Jason, Lisa, Kimberley, Pam, and Jennifer along with their mother goose.

Comforting HONKS to the special goslings that were injured and had to drop out of the formation until they could rejoin the flight: Patti, Amy, Terri, Enetrice, Ellen, and Mary.

I found myself in the midst of historic turbulence during this flight, but felt it was vital to see this book "MOTHER GOOSE" reaches a destination that just might touch the hearts of the 18 families who lost their precious loved ones that were once in our migration. This Mother Goose still mourns their absence. I miss them too.

To those of you who gave your incredible endorsements, representing years of special friendship, you deserve enormous HONKS. You gave me confidence and encouragement with your impressive endorsements that appear in "MOTHER GOOSE". Your good wishes gave me the incentive to keep the course and finish the flight. Thank you.

Also deserving huge HONKS were many of you, friends, family members, and acquaintances, who crossed my path and greeted me with anticipation when you would ask "how's the book coming" or "can't wait to read your book." Thanks to all of you! You know who you are.

I have many grateful HONKS for my son Terry Rose and his remarkable memory that I called on many times during the process of writing and editing "MOTHER GOOSE". He sometimes even had to make house calls when my computer had navigation flight-path problems; or when I ran into turbulence through this journey as I recalled some of the darkest days.

I was blessed and was kept grounded with my own little flock during this journey: Son Jerry and wife Barbara, son

Terry and wife Ginna, 3 grandchildren: Chad, Amanda and David, and 5 "little greats". One little great left us for a new destination (Heaven) when he was only eight months old.

Gigantic HONKS to Princella who assisted research, typing and with the lovely book cover of "MOTHER GOOSE". Her editorial skills gave me great self-assurance and reinforcement, and always made me feel that my book was as important to her as it was to me Thank you, Princella.

About the Author
Florence Rogers

Florence views the building dedication plaque presented to her at the Allegiance Federal Credit Union formerly known as the Federal Employees Credit Union.

Florence Rogers was hired by Federal Employees Credit Union (FECU) April 1, 1971 as the CEO and stayed until her retirement in 1997.

She was present at her office on April 19, 1995 when it was destroyed in the Oklahoma City Bombing, and she lost 18 of her staff of 33 in the disaster. Florence and six surviving staff members were instrumental in the recovery of the credit union that opened up 48 hours after the tragedy.

During her tenure with the FECU, Florence was elected as the first woman Board Chairman of the Oklahoma Credit Union League; inducted into the Credit Union Executives Society (CUES) Hall of Fame; voted Oklahoma's Professional of the Year; inducted into the Cornerstone Credit Union League Hall of Fame; and received a Citation of Honor as a Distinguished Oklahoma Recipient from the State of Oklahoma.

Florence has traveled extensively throughout the United States and internationally to Canada, Australia, and Kenya, Africa telling her story of survival and giving disaster recovery presentations.

After retirement, she remained involved with the OKC National Memorial, her neighborhood Association, the Cleveland County Election Board, family reunions and her church. Florence is the mother to two sons, Jerry and Terry Rose, and enjoys her family, helping others, making greeting cards and scrapbooking.

Series Creator & Co-Author *Princella D. Smith*

Princella Smith is a Regional Emmy-nominated director, producer, author, and media personality.

She is the creator and co-author of the Beauty for Ashes (BFA) Book Series about survivors and first responders of the Oklahoma City Bombing.

Princella formerly served as a political strategist having worked as a Communications Director on Capitol Hill in Washington, DC and for several high profile elected officials and political figures. Her political media experience includes numerous features on various national outlets as a political commentator and more prominently as a prime time speaker at the 2004 Republican National Convention in Madison Square Garden in New York City. At the time, Princella was two months shy of her 21st birthday and was also afforded the opportunity to be the Official Greeter for President and Mrs. George W. & Laura Bush and Secretary of State, Condoleezza Rice.

In 2019, Princella wrote, produced, and directed an Oklahoma City Bombing-themed Public Service Announcement (PSA) titled "The World Watched" on behalf of the two organizations, Survive First and Healthy Hire Healthy Retire, promoting PTSD treatment in first responders.

The PSA garnered a 2020 Boston / New England Regional Emmy nomination and a Communicator Award of Distinction from the Academy of Interactive and Visual Arts.

Princella received a B.A. in Political Science from Ouachita Baptist University in Arkansas. She studied for a master's degree in Counter-Terrorism and Homeland Security at the Lauder School of Government at the Interdisciplinary Center, a private research college in Herzliya, Israel.

Princella is a native of Arkansas currently residing in the State of Tennessee.

Photo Gallery

A day at the office during my tenure as CEO of the Federal Employees Credit Union.

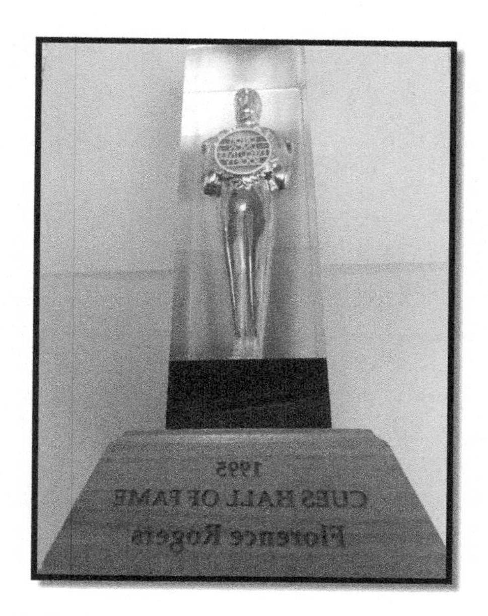

Hall of Fame Trophy awarded by the Credit Union Executives Society (CUES).

Induction into the Cornerstone Credit Union League Hall of Fame.

Exchange between survivors and family members of the Oklahoma City Bombing and the United States embassy bombings in Kenya.

Girlfriend, my loyal dog. What a personality this pup had! She was a great companion in tough times.

One of several professional photos taken for the Federal Employees Credit Union. I was known for my distinctive red hair.

High School Senior Photo

OKLAHOMA BANKING DEPARTMENT RESOLUTION

**A RESOLUTION COMMENDING THE EFFORTS
OF FLORENCE ROGERS
FOR HER YEARS OF SERVICE
TO THE OKLAHOMA CREDIT UNION COMMUNITY**

WHEREAS, Florence Rogers has devoted her time and dedication to the development of the Oklahoma Credit Union Community.

WHEREAS, Florence Rogers is well-liked and respected in the credit union industry.

WHEREAS, the Oklahoma Banking Department wishes to express its appreciation to Florence Rogers for her years of service to the credit union members of Oklahoma.

NOW, THEREFORE, BE IT RESOLVED BY THE OKLAHOMA BANKING COMMISSIONER:

THAT, Florence Rogers be acknowledged and commended for her outstanding contributions and accomplishments.

THAT, a copy of this resolution be distributed to Florence Rogers and the Oklahoma State Credit Union Board.

Adopted by the Oklahoma Banking Commissioner on the 26th day of June, 1997.

Mick Thompson, Commissioner

Citation of Honor as a Distinguished Oklahoma Recipient from the State of Oklahoma presented when I was inducted into the Cornerstone Credit Union League Hall of Fame.

Mother Goose

Saying goodbye to the flock at my retirement party.

Carefree days of youth in Minco, Oklahoma.
What a circle life has been!

Our little family back in Minco, Oklahoma. Me (far left in polka dots); younger sister, Joellyn (front center in white dress); brothers Bobby (back row left) & Don (back row right); mother, Lucy and Father, Lee (center).

Made in the USA
Las Vegas, NV
15 September 2022